AFRICA PRESENTS THE CONGO RDC

AND

EXPERIENCE OF TWO YOUNG AFRICAN LADIES

IN AMERICA

BY

Bepona Collection

AFRICA presents the CONGO RDC

and

Two African Young Ladies in AMERICA.

BEPONA COLLECTION

FIRST EDITION

Copyright © 2011 by *BEPONA COLLECTION*

ISBN: 978-0-9859230-6-8

Printed in the United of America

BeponaBooks

AFRICA

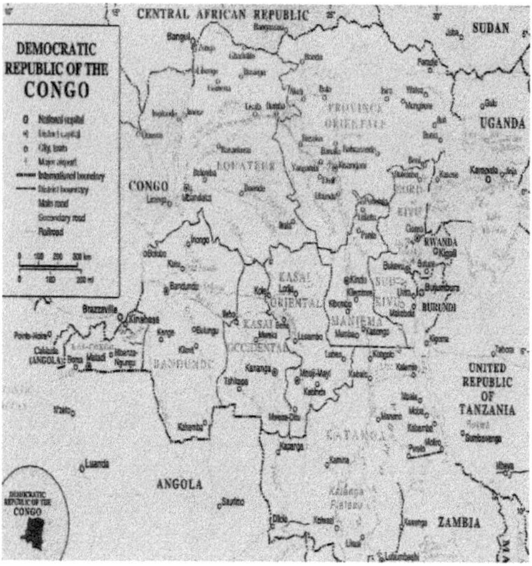

DEMOCRATIC REPUBLIC OF THE CONGO
CENTRAL AFRICAN REPUBLIC
SUDAN
UGANDA
CONGO
RWANDA
BURUNDI
UNITED REPUBLIC OF TANZANIA
ANGOLA
ZAMBIA
Brazzaville
Kinshasa
Luanda
KASAI ORIENTAL
MANIEMA
KATANGA
Main road
Secondary road
Railroad

KINSHASA, *THE CAPITAL CITY OF THE CONGO, RDC*

PRIOR TO THE CIVIL WAR

CONTENTS

Chapter VI

Chapter VII

Chapter VIII

Chapter IX

INTRODUCTION

Generally, everyone who had traveled in the foreign land should be familiar with disadvantage or misfortune which the newcomers may encounter while sojourning in the foreign land. Sometimes, attempting to associate with the so called countrymen does not always bring a positive experience.

Meeting with the compatriots who had been established in the foreign land could bring some degree of advantage. However at times, it could bring a high degree of disadvantage. It is advantageous, when your fellow citizens who had been settled in that land are willing to guide you towards a positive direction.

Further, it is preferable if those individuals are honest enough to keep the newcomer out of trouble, and prevent wrong people approaching that individual, which could possibly result to a chaotic situation such as, confiscating the individual's personal belongings or harming that person all together. Nonetheless, when the countrymen turn out to be malicious, they have tendency to approach the newcomers cunningly, and eventually take advantage of them.

We shall see how Mr. Magoke dealt with the two young African ladies from his home town.

Basically, in the world, some individuals or guests have propensity of sometimes making, wonderful promises to their hosts and their family members, especially to their children if they have any. This happens especially if the host's hospitality exceeded their expectations; so out of that excitement, the guests would wind up making promises, which might be beyond their abilities to fulfill. However, once they depart from the host's view or home, so often, they tend to forget their obligations, and as a result, they would fail utterly to keep their promises. So often, such situation occurs especially, when those individuals do not anticipate any further encounter, which might necessitate confrontations in the future.

Evidently, no individual could escape the world's challenges. And no one can possibly predict what types of people they might meet in the future, whether in their own country or abroad. We would like to invite our readers to travel with us in this book and notice what the world is all about.

CHAPITER - I

Meeting the Two Young Ladies

Bipake and Lunungi were female High School graduate from the Democratic Republic of the Congo, in central Africa. They were eighteen years old and graduated from the most reputable High School of their country, which was called Lyceum, "Institut Politechnique Congolaise." Due to the higher reputation of that School, its tuition cost was eventually exorbitant for an average family to be able to effort it. In the light of this, only children whom parents exhibited sound financial statuses could attend that School, whereas those who came from modest families remained admirers or spectators of the Lyceum's students. Apparently, both young ladies felt fortunate indeed to be born from such privileged families.

Because Bipake and Lunungi were very bright students, the school awarded them scholarships in order to pursue their higher education in Belgium. And this was based upon diplomatic relationships, which both countries had actually established. Regardless to the opportunity offered them, both young ladies declined the awards; and chose rather to pursue their college education in the United States of America, because their families' acquaintances had previously advised them that doing so, would help them tremendously in improving their English; and ultimately, they would become proficient.

At first, when that concept had reached their parents' ears, they had showed a high degree of reluctance, prior to agreeing with the young ladies' decision. Ultimately, the parents consented with the advice received from their business associates, Mr. Zariap and Mr. Zolog. Apparently, the young ladies' families had no slightest concept regarding Colleges education's expenses in America, because they were so accustomed in financing some of their children's education with the Belgium's currency in Brussels.

In fact, having been colonized by Belgium, many Congolese parents had formed the habit of sending their children to pursue their education in Brussels, Belgium, because the education expenses were moderate and almost similar with that in the Congo; and so was the school program at that particular time. Similarly, there were many Belgian and other foreign students who chose to pursue their University education at Lovanium University of Congo at that time, as well.

Apparently, the yearly expense in the boarding school where Bipake and Lunungi spent six years of their Secondary education was quite similar to the one in Belgium. Therefore, their families felt confident at first that they could also afford to finance their children's college expense in the United States of America with the same amount of money. Ultimately, the cost exceeded their anticipation.

Previously, Mr. Bipake and Mr. Lunungi both had worked in private sectors. However, subsequently, they became self-employers in the long run; and then, they formed a partnership. They were specialized in precious stones business and became very successful businessmen. Being that their daughters had to travel abroad, each parent made a serious preparation for his daughter's travels to the United States of America. For that reason, each parent decided to offer his daughter an allowance in the amount of $ 5,000.00 (five thousands) inittially. In addition, each of them was also given a good quantity of assorted germs (semi precious stones) worth about $10,000 (ten thousand dollars) based on the market price at that time.

Meeting Mr. David Zariap and Abraham Mr. Rolog

Mr. Zariap and Rolog were businessmen as well. They had formed the habit of traveling to Congo in order to establish a business partnership with Mr. Bipake and Mr. Lunungi. In fact, they had come several times in order to re –inforce their business relationship, and also to finalize ultimately their business transactions or contract.. Basically, the relationship between Mr. David Zariap, Mr. Abraham Rolog from America and Mr. Bipake and Mr. Lunungi from the Congo began since1968 when David Zariap and Abraham Rolog went to Congo in search of Business partners who were engaged in precious stone business.

Unfortunately, both parties had a language problem. On one hand, Mr. Bipake and Mr. Lunungi spoke French and very little English. On the other hand, Mr. Zariap and Rolog spoke English and very limited French, which made it eventually very difficult to finalize their business deals. However, they were privileged at least to have Miss Bipake and Miss Lunungi, who had acquired some knowledge of the English language.

It was quite a propos during that time, because the school's regulations had finally approved for senior high school students, to be offered at least one hour per week of English course. Because of their level of English, even though minor, both young ladies had been able to render a great deal of service to their respective fathers and their business associates; attempting to assist their parents during their business meetings. They were actually attempting to stretch their hearing muscles to be able to understand the American accent, which sounded different from that of their high school English teacher. She was the native of Belgium, and precisely from the Southern part of Belgium. Apparently, her English sounded quite different from that of Mr. Zariap and Mr. Rolog. One could immediately detect her French accent whenever their English teacher spoke, and especially in the pronunciation of the letter "*R*" and in the words, "*The*, or *That*."

Obviously both, Congolese and American parties used to face some sort of difficulties in terms of conducting their business discussions, while the young ladies were not on their weekend break from the boarding school. Nevertheless, sometimes, the time was not appropriate for them to leave the boarding school in order to attend their parents' business meeting. The school policy could not authorize any student to go out of the boarding school more than once a month.

And for this reason, both parties would experience some inconvenience to have a successful business transactions, during the time that the young ladies would actually be at the boarding school. In the light of this, both parties began to schedule their business meetings, based on the young ladies' boarding school's break or schedule.

Obviously, the Lyceum's regulations were very strict, and therefore, students and their parents had to adhere or respect the school regulations once that student has been admitted. In addition, it was very difficult around that time to encounter any individual who was bilingual, French-English who could ensure interpretation service in the capital city of Kinshasa, because French has always been the national language, and Flemish, according to the board of education was placed as a second language in the country. English language was not permitted at the early years until the student had actually reached senior level. This arrangement had been so, due to the fact that Belgium is known as a bilingual country, French-Flemish; and therefore, the same system was instituted in their previous colony.

Basically, both Zariap and Rolog used to travel to Kinshasa once every two months, and at that time, Bipake and Lunungi would be out of the boarding School in order to spend a weekend with their respective families. Mr. Bipake and Lunungi would therefore seize that opportunity to invite their daughters to have dinner with them and their business associates in order to ensure the interpretation in both languages, English-French. That association had certainly facilitated the social contact of their daughters with their prospective business partners.

Zariap and Rolog had always been excited whenever the two young ladies would be present while the meeting was being conducted. The students would utilize all their abilities to interpret back and forth, especially Miss Bipake, she was bold, and endeavored to pronounce even the most difficult English word, she enjoyed leaning English in class, and had always been the best student in her class as well, whereas Miss Lunungi appeared to be bashful, apparently, she was afraid to make a mistake in her pronunciation. It was noticed that every time the girls would attend the partners' meeting, the outcome would be successful.

In effect, Mr. Bipake and Lunungi had always considered Zariap and Rolog as their guests of honor, and therefore, they were always taken to the most exclusive restaurant of the City. Mr. Bipake and Mr. Lunungi would always pay for the restaurants' expenses.

Sometimes however, the meetings would be conducted either at Mr. Bipak's or Mr. Ludungi's residence. Both had huge homes in the borough of Limete, which was known to be a very refine borough at that time. The meals would also be served. The atmosphere had always been joyous or cheerful, and the business discussions would be conducted harmoniously. In fact, it had been during those occasions that Mr. Zariap and Mr. Rolog had developed the habit of advising Miss Bipake and Miss Lunungi to consider coming to United State of America in order to pursue their college education, and eventually improve their English. They used to say it right in front of their parents. They had mentioned it repeatedly until both young ladies began picturing it in their minds and accepted it fully. Eventually, it became a reality right after their graduation.

Mr. Zariap and Rolog had given the young ladies and their families such a very good impressions of themselves. Effectively, they had appeared trustworthy people in the eyes of their hosts. Evidently, to their end, Zariap and Rolog were quite aware that Mr. Bipake and Lunungi were financially sound, and therefore they were capable to support their own daughters in America, based on what they had viewed around them.

In a few occasions, the issue of allowing those young ladies to go and study in America alone was raised at the dinner table. After debating it, however, both Mr. Bipake and Lunungi had showed some degree of objection, because America was so far away from home, and especially for the fact that they had nobody or a guarantor over there to assist the girls, should any problem occurs. Mr. Bipake appeared to be more pessimistic than Mr. Lunungi. Mr. Zariap and Rolog, would reply, "We actually do not see any inconvenience or difference, once the girls leave your country and go abroad, whether they go to Brussels, or to America, you, as parents will not be accompanying them, anyway. Why don't you just be relaxed and let them come to America, where they could acquire a better education and become fluent in English?" Mr. Bipake would answer that, it is actually a matter of habit. We Congolese people are so accustomed to sending our children to Brussels. Because we have the same time zone that facilitates us to communicate at any time we choose, and this grant us some degree of consolation. This makes us actually feel as though we are close to each other, laughter!

In addition, based on our business activities, said Mr. Bipake, we travel there on a regular basis as well. Therefore, sending two young ladies in a foreign land, such as your huge country would actually be very hard for us, and especially for their mothers, as you know, female gender is very emotional, and attempting to convince them would be like pulling a tooth out of their mouths, replied Mr. Bipake, laughter!" Why is that?" Mr. Rolog asked him right after that. To that question, Mr. Lunungi replied, "it is a simple fact that we actually have nobody there, who could bring them any assistance, on a regular basis; you see our point?"

In this regard, both Zariap and Rolog replied, "Well, now that all of us have established a very close association together, such concern should actually be dissipated from your feelings." Moreover, both gentlemen assured both Mr. Bipake and Lunungi that, "Our respective residences are located in New York City as you know. Rolog and I would make sure to bring assistance to the girls if they do come to study in New York City. We will find them a good school and an apartment in a very nice neighborhood, which will be similar to the borough of *"LIMETE."* We are quite aware that the girls are so accustomed to living in a refined borough and homes; and surely, they would be very delighted there as well, confirmed Mr. Zariap."

During their last trip to Kinshasa, all of them were gathered at the dinner table in that exclusive restaurant at *MONT-GALIEMA* area.

While they were having lunch, Mr. Zariap eagerly voiced the following words to the young ladies, "It would be our pleasure to help you out if you come to America, girls!. Don't be frightened. It is actually a normal reaction, traveling in the foreign land for the first time causes a high degree of anxiety. Zariap looked at Rolog, and laughed loud. Zariap said, "The reason we are now laughing is due to the fact that we too at first had been afraid to travel to Africa. Because we had such a negative image of the people and the country we were planning to go to. No one can really anticipate what to expect in the foreign land, when traveling for the first time. See, how things had turned out for us now? We are glad indeed that we took the initiatives to come, and meet with you, "Zariap concluded.

Rolog advised them that you girls may also wind up having a wonderful experience in our country. However, if you do decide to come to America, you should actually notify us earlier than your departure date, so that we can be able to make appropriate accommodations for you. Further, we will also arrange our schedule in order to come and pick you up at the airport. That actually should not be any problem for us. All we will have to do is to adjust our business schedule, he added.

Mr. Rolog confirmed that, actually we will be there in person to greet you, so that you do not feel lost in the foreign land, and especially in a huge city such as New York City," laughter!

Furthermore, Mr. Rolog said, "In fact, if you plan to come for the upcoming academic year, just remember to come early, because you will need to register for ESL course. Furthermore, he explained the "ESL" is the English Course which all the foreign students need to take prior to beginning their College education." Many questions were revolved around this statement, and apparently, they were all clarified. Because of that reassurance, both Mr. Bipake and Lunungi including their daughters were uplifted, and got all excited, and then, began to *take this matter very seriously*. Both of their respective mothers were also convinced that all would go well, seeing the presence of Zariap and Rolog around their homes.

In fact, at the closing of their last trip in the Congo, Mr. Rolog had borrowed $200 from Mr. Bipake in exchange with his personal check in the amount of $200.00. He had actually assured Mr. Bipake, not to worry about accepting his personal check, because he had enough fund to cover the amount that was written.

Additionally he explained to him that the reason he needed that money urgently at that time, was to offer the gratuities to the hotel maids for having rendered him such a great service. In addition, Rolog advised Mr. Bipake to deposit the check in his account immediately, and it was going to be cleared without any delay. As instructed, with no doubt, Mr. Bipake deposited it, and withdrew the same amount of money to give to his daughter who needed to pay for her ferry ticket to Brazzaville. Fifteen days later however, Mr. Bipake's bank returned a check stamped, "*NSF*" from Mr. Rolog's bank. In addition, it was also stated that, "this account had already been closed." The girls did witness that incident. Naturally, it was viewed to be unpleasant and discouraging to all of them. Why had Mr. Rolog written a check from the account which had already been closed? That was obviously quite a big puzzle to both fathers and their daughters.

Nevertheless, five months prior to travelling, Mr. Zariap and Rolog were called and notified that both families had converged and the decision was made for both Bipake and Lunungi to travel to America as per their advice. All the travel information , or the itineraries were clarified and communicated to both Rolog and Zariap. And both of them had acknowledged receipt of the information that was sent to them. Certainly, they knew that the young ladies shall be arriving within five months as it was indicated, unless they notify us otherwise.

CHAPTER II

Bipake and Lunungi traveled to the Foreign Land

Moreover, three days prior to Bipake and Lunungi's trip abroad, their fathers' meeting in Brussels was called to order. It was such a coincidence, because all of them were obligated to travel the same day due to the fact that their respective fathers had to attend their business meeting with their business associates in Brussels, as well. It had turned out to be such a wonderful coincidence indeed for all of them to travel in the Congo Airways, from Kinshasa to Brussels. Zariap and Rolog had been called to confirm the actual departure. Rolog and Zariap were quite familiar with the itineraries, because they, themselves had been travelling constantly and had always followed similar itineraries, and sometimes via Sabena Airlines.

After arriving in Brussels, Mr. Bipake and Lunungi called Zariap and Rolog in order to confirm their arrival in Brussels, and also to re-confirm their daughters' departure from Brussels to New York City. Their reply to that re-confirmation had been, "very well and thank you for the reminder. There will be no problem since the arrival date remained the same; the girls should not be frightened.

Everything has already been taken care of. We will definitely be at the airport to pick them up, Zariap confirmed. Because Mr. Bipake and Ludungi were somewhat nervous regarding their daughters' trip to the foreign land, for the first time alone; and especially due to the lack of a close family member to ensure assistance, should any urgent need arise.

Mr. Lunungi was full of anxiety on that departure's day. Half an hour later, he decided to call Mr. Zariap again, and he said: "By the way, please take down the girls' itineraries once more, in case you had misplaced the previous information that was given to you previously. Mr. Ludungi read the itineraries once more to Mr. Zariap: "The girls will be departing from Brussels to New York City by Sabena Airlines, which will be arriving in New York City on Friday at 9:00 p.m. – Again, Mr. Zariap, replied, "Oh, Bipake, relaxed, you are full of anxiety, stop being so frightened. We know that we will have to pick them up at the Kennedy Airport." This reassurance made Mr. Bipake and Lunungi, and their daughters extremely happy. They did not have to worry, since everything was in readiness, an apartment or hotel accommodation surely had been arranged, so they thought.

An hour prior to the girls' departure, Mr. Bipake and Lunungi had once again spoken with both gentlemen Zariap and Mr. Rolof in order to re-confirm their daughters' departure and arrival to their destination. Again, Mr. Zariap and Rolog confirmed that they will be available to pick them up from the airport. They reminded them, "please do not be alarmed. That is nothing, but a minor issue," Zariap added.

What would our readers conclude in regard to this issue? Was it a scheme or Zariap and Rolog had just wanted to mock them in order to satisfy their frustration for not being successful in convincing their partners to sign that business deal? Dismayed as it were, when both young ladies had arrived at the airport, it was quite a surprise; and a very bad surprised indeed to them.

Zariap and Rolof did not show up to pick them up as they had actually promised. Because they were not present, both young ladies took out of the purses, Mr. Zariap and Mr. Rolog's business cards which were given to them while they came in the Congo. And then, they walked towards a public phone. Since they had no coins to place the phone call, Bipake reached in her purse and took out a five dollar bill. She then turned to face the people standing around her.

And then, she asked a gentleman who was standing close by, "Sir, can you possibly exchange this $5.00 bill and That gentleman was kind enough to break that five dollars bill and he provided her with few coins. Right after receiving the coins, Bipake dialed Zariap phone number. After two rings, somebody answered the phone, and replied, "Hello! This is Zariap, how may I help you?" It was Mr. Zariap's well known voice. Miss Bipake replied "Hello, Mr. Zariap, this is Bipake and Lunungi; we have finally landed at Kennedy airport. Can you come to pick us up?" Surprisingly, as it were, immediately, Mr. Zariap changed his voice and replied, "Well, I am sorry, Zariap is not here at the moment. He is away, on a long weekend.

Here in America, the gentleman continued, our weekend actually begins on a Friday and ends up on Monday morning." Oh, who are you anyway, he asked?" Bipake then repeated, "I am Bipake the daughter of Mr. Bipake whom you met in the Congo, one of your business associates. I am with my girlfriend Lunungi, the daughter of Mr. Lunungi, your business partner as well." Miss Bipake made an attempt to convince the man on the phone. Unfortunately, Mr. Zariap continued to pretend as though he had never heard of those two Congolese names before. He replied, saying, "Oh, unfortunately, Mr. Zariap is not here.

He repeated once more, "Here in America, our weekends actually begin on Fridays. Today is Friday, Mr. Zariap and his family are away. They shall return on Monday, O.k., sorry!"

Shortly after saying these words, he immediately, hanged up the phone. Bipake and Lunungi stood there at the airport. Naturally, they were discouraged, nervous and puzzled. They were disoriented, the fact that they had no direction to follow from that point on. Each one of them had a big luggage, a medium size handbag, and a small purse.

Both young ladies had a minimum knowledge of the English language, which they had learned for two semesters from their High School back home. Their comprehension was pretty fair. They stated that they could understand fairly well and communicate with any individual who spoke clearly, or proper English such as Mr. Zariap and Rolog, but had difficulties trying to communicate with those who used slang idioms at the airport. Consequently, they were puzzled, and they stopped to think for awhile, how they were going to proceed under such circumstance?

Fortunately, while they were standing around the public telephone at the airport, they perceived three gentlemen. They were apparently the airport workers; because they were pushing luggage carriers.

The gentlemen were quite impressed to notice how attractive both young ladies appeared. They were dressed up in their African outfits, and apparently, it was what African themselves referred to as the Congolese refined style.

Further, they gentlemen noticed that they were wearing expensive jewelries and watches. One could tell at a glance that they were from a high class families. Each of them had a lot of hair, groomed in afro style, but their hair appeared slightly pressed, apparently with a hot comb. Bipake appeared five feet eight tall, and weighed probably around one hundred thirty pounds. Lunungi appeared five feet four and weighed around one hundred twenty pounds.

Suddenly, one of the gentlemen approached them courageously, and asked them in English, "Ladies, do you need help to carry your luggage out?" Bipake was the outspoken and responded right away, "No, thank you. We actually are tying to reach the people who were supposed to pick us up tonight.

The Gentleman seized the opportunity to ask them, "Which country are you from ladies?" Bipake replied right away, "We are from the Democratic Republic of Congo."

The gentleman exclaimed, "Oh, I see you are from the Belgium Congo?" Lunungi made a quick correction right then, "No, Congo is now an independent country. It is no longer called Belgium Congo. It is rather called Democratic Republic of Congo."

The gentleman apologized for his ignorance. Then he continued, "I realize that you ladies speak French. All of a sudden, both of them replied, "yes we do." The gentleman smiled at them, and added, so do I. Shortly after that, he began to speak with them in French. He introduced himself as *Pierrot Malsain*. The girls were really amazed, and Bipake said: "We didn't know that French is spoken in this country as well. What a pleasure!" She added.

Pierrot continued, "Actually, I am a Haitian descendant, born in Haiti and raised in Brooklyn. I am just a temporary employee here at this airport; I work as a luggage carrier as you notice. As I have indicated previously, I am here on a temporary basis, because I am a reserved military. Soon, I will be called to return abroad in the service." Bipake and Lunungi were happy to meet a person who was bilingual; certainly he could assist them to reach Zariap and Rolog. That was their main concern.

How can I assist you ladies? He asked them. Bipake pulled out Zariap and Rolog's business cards, and showed it to Pierrot. He held it, and then he began to dial Zariap's number. All of a sudden, a gentleman answered the phone. Suddenly, Pierrot asked to speak with Mr. Zariap.

And then, Zariap replied this he, who are you? Pierrot answered: "I am actually calling from the airport, we have two young ladies here from the Congo, who are waiting to be picked up by you, and so they said. Are you coming to pick them up or what seems to be the story?" Hearing this statement, the gentleman, right away changed the subject. He replied: "Well, actually I am not Zariap. Zariap is away on a weekend. He will be back on Monday." Pierrot realized that the man was unwilling to come to the airport, and assist the young ladies. He suddenly replied, "Sir, didn't you just answer me a moment ago, confirming that, *THIS IS HE*?" Zariap replied sarcastically, "excuse me sir, do you speak English? What did I just say? I have just told you that Zariap is not here, O.K.?" Having said those words, he then hanged up the phone, once more.. At that particular moment, Pierrot's co-workers, and the two young ladies were facing Pierrot. And eventually, they were following the conversation.

Evidently, Pierrot was convinced that the so called Mr. Zariap was not a reliable individual. He felt badly, and could not explain Zariap's negative reaction over the phone to those who were standing there. He chose to make it sound mild. As a result, he twisted the things around, and said: "Zariap actually went to spend his weekend somewhere else. He will return Monday." Lunungi, said: "Can you possibly dial Mr. Rolog number he probably is available."

Pierrot dialed Rolog's phone number. Then Rolog answered the phone, "this is **Rolog**, may I help you?" Pierrot greeted him, "Hello, Mr. Rolog my name is Pierrot Malsain. The man repeated, Pierrot Malsain? Who are you?" He continued to ask. Pierrot replied, "I am actually calling from Kennedy airport. There are two young ladies here at the airport waiting for you to pick them up. They have already arrived in case you forgot your schedule," he added. Rolog grew nasty over the phone. And then he said: "You just hang up that phone man, and don't you ever call my house again," he had said it sarcastically!

Pierrot told the young ladies, "Excuse me for a second. He then approached his co-workers who where standing few steps away from the young ladies.

He said to them, "I really feel badly about these young ladies. Both gentlemen are playing a trick on them. Apparently they are not going to pick them up. Three of those gentlemen felt badly as well for the young ladies who apparently knew nobody else in New York City.

One of the gentlemen told Pierrot, asked them how in the world they actually receive Zariap and Rolog's business cards, in the first place? Lunungi replied they are actually our fathers' business associates. They came to Congo in a regular basis. They always had dinner with us whenever they came for business meeting in the Congo with our fathers. Lunungi explained in details. Then Pierrot asked them, "What is the purpose of your visit here, anyway?" Bipake answered this time, saying: "The purpose of our visit here is to pursue our college education in English. Zariap and Rolog had advised our respective fathers that American's education is the best in the World; and that it would help us to understand and speak English fluently."

Bipake continued, Lunungi and I did very well in high school. We both in fact had been awarded each a scholarship to study in Europe.

Unfortunately each of us declined it, because Zariap and Rolog convinced my father and Lunungi's father that your daughters would acquire an extensive knowledge studying in America rather than studying in Europe.

Pierrot would stop every now and then, to actually explain to his colleagues who could not understand French or comprehend the girls' narrative. Then, Pierrot would resume asking more questions in order to assess the whole situation. He continued, so what did Zariap and Rolog actually tell your fathers while in Congo, and in connection with you coming in this country? Bipake replied, "every time that we were at the dinner table home, Zariap and Rolog expressed their willingness to assist Lunungi and myself in finding the best school in the city, and in making arrangement of our housing accommodations.

One of the Pierrot co-workers suggested another question. He told Pierrot to ask the young ladies that, "when actually was the last time they had spoken with Zariap and Rolog?" So, Pierrot did. Both responded in unison, "Well, it was actually yesterday, Thursday at 10:00 a.m., New York time. Our fathers' had a long conversation with them over the phone while we were in Brussels. Our entire itinerary was confirmed and communicated to them. They knew our departure time from Brussels via Sabena Airlines. All our flights information was given to them. Bipake and I myself did say hello to them over the phone as well. Their last word to us had actually been, "We see you tomorrow, and welcome to New York!" So we really don't quite understand why they aren't here to pick us up, as they actually confirmed. This whole scenario seems peculiar, she added. They are not teenagers to want play boyish pranks; both are in their late fifties.

Hearing this, Pierrot, shook his head, looking at his colleagues, then he said: "Apparently those people were not sincere. How can people be so deceitful! Why confirm an action which you know would be impossible to perform? They said to each other, "What are the young ladies planning to do now in this kind of situation? Pierrot translated the question to both young ladies, saying to them "Being that your sponsors are not available to assist you, what are your immediate plans?" It was getting very late, nearly two o'clock in the morning. Bipake and Lunungi asked Pierrot: "Can you please recommend a hotel where we can stay during this entire weekend until Monday morning when we will make further attempt to reach Zariap and Rolog by then?"

He said, "There are few hotels around here which I can actually recommend, but do you have any money on you?" Pierrot asked them. The young ladies confirmed that they did actually have money. Pierrot and his colleagues loaded belongings on the luggage carrier, and brought them at the taxi stand. The first thing that Pierrot did was to call 'International Hotel which is located around the airport in order to inquire about a room's availability. After receiving hotel's confirmation, subsequently, Pierrot went out and then stopped a yellow taxi. He told the taxi man to take the young ladies to the International Hotel. Prior to getting in the taxi, Bipake and Lunungi tipped Pierrot fifteen dollars for all the help he had actually rendered them. Pierrot was thankful, and gave them his telephone number in case they needed any further assistance.

They had waited until the following Monday to re-try calling Zariap once more. Bipake and Lunungi had made several attempts in reaching Zariap by phone, on that particular Monday. They had noticed, however that the phone sounded always busy. Eventually, they gave him a benefit of the doubt, probably being a potential businessman he could possibly be on the phone, dealing with his business associates abroad.

Since the girls were unable to reach Zariap and his friend on that Monday, the girls rushed to call the hotel where their fathers' business meeting was being held in Brussels. Nevertheless, the meeting was over, and they had already checked out. While they had been in transit in Brussels, the girls met the hotel concierge. They decided to speak with him personally in order to inquire whether or not their fathers had actually checked out of the Hotel.

The concierge was a Frenchman called **Claude Morondière**. Because Bipake and Lunungi stayed ten days in that Hotel assisting their fathers and the secretary in organizing business meetings, and at the same time, they were also waiting for their departure day to the USA. Mr. Morondière knew them well, and had been very helpful to them. Morondière also knew that both young ladies were going to the United State in order to pursue their college education. Therefore, as soon as Bipake requested to speak with him, he was overwhelmed to hear her voice from the United States. He had never had an opportunity to visit the United States of America.

Claude was just excited, and started to ask various questions about New York City, and its tall buildings. He also questioned about his favorite gospel music and singers.

He went on and on, however he had no slightest concept that Bipake and her friend were facing a serious challenge in New York City. Bipake decided to interrupt his excitement and asked Mr. Morondière, "Please tell me whether or not my father Bipake and Mr. Lunungi are still the guests at your Hotel?" Claude Morondière answered that, unfortunately, Miss Bipake, your father and Mr. Lunungi checked out on Saturday at 12 p.m. I think they should be on their way back to Congo," he replied. So Miss Bipake, thanked him, and had to cut the conversation short.

However, prior to bidding him goodbye, Claude Morondière said to Bipake, "Excuse me Miss Bipake; I really love American gospel music. I would appreciate it very much if you can start sending me at least three records a month, whenever you are settled down. I know you can afford it," he said with conviction. He continued your father and Mr. Lunungi are really gentlemen! The gratuities they left everyone here is really appreciated. Everyone is so grateful.

Every worker told them that whenever they come back next time to conduct another meeting in Brussels, they should make sure to come and stay in our hotel."

After ending the conversation with Monrondière, Bipake turned to her girl-friend Lunungi, sadly, and said to her, shaking her head: "Guess what? They have just left Brussels. They should be en route back to Congo, right now." Well, Lunungi replied desolately, "I guess we will have to remain in this hotel until we reach them for further instructions eventually." Bipake added, well, today is Tuesday; if they left this evening, they will arrive eventually tomorrow morning. And therefore, we must continue to call home until we will reach them, because we have no other alternatives here in the foreign land.

Lunungi continued I hope they are heading directly to Kinshasa, and that they are not going to Bukavu city (the eastern part of the country), as they had initially planned. The girls were frantic indeed. This would mean that we would have to be stationed here at the International Hotel until we are able to establish a communication with our families. Naturally so, replied Lunungi, because they do not know our whereabouts. They probably are so relaxed, thinking that we are in the good hands of their so called business associates. But Bipake noted, knowing how anxious the families had actually been prior to our departure to so far away from home, our mothers and the rest of the family should probably be devastated at this point, not being able to reach us, since we have left Brussels.

Lunungi commented that knowing my father, they probably had tried to call Zariap and Rolog several time in order to inquire about our whereabouts All of them will surely be dismayed to hear the tricks which Zariap and Rolog had actually played against us. It is heartbreaking experience, because we all regarded them highly.

Bipake and Lunungi looked at each other, and could hardly believe that Mr. Zariap and Rolog were really the same individuals who used to have lunches and dinners in the exclusive restaurants in the Congo with their parents, and sometimes in their respective homes with them together with their families.

Further the girls began to recall the number of times they had accompanied their fathers in their big Cadillac to pick up and drop both Mr. Zariap and Mr. Rolog from and to MemLing Hotel in Kinshasa, where they used to stay. The young ladies remembered also how both individuals appeared to have a happy demeanor and exhibited such a good sense of humors while they were in the Congo. It is just incredible to notice how bloody cold they actually were once they have arrived in New York City. This was just shocking to the young ladies.

Bipake said to Lunungi, thank God that we both have money, and we also have our semi precious stones to sell in case we run out of cash. Lunungi replied, "The only thing we would need is to find out the location where we can possibly sell our stones. Further, we would need an honest person who can clearly inform us regarding the current market price of the stones. Bipake answered back, "I am pretty sure that God will always bring forth somebody to assist us in this matter. We should just hold on into it for the time being that we still have cash in hand. The young ladies, having parents who were business oriented, were somewhat very knowledgeable of certain business aspects. They were alert and complementary of each other in terms of their decision making.

The Young ladies Established Communication with Hotel Chambermaids

Bipake and Lunungi continued to stay at the International Hotel. During all their stay in the hotel, they had formed the habit of requesting room service rather than walking to the hotel restaurant. They were so accustomed dealing with room service in the hotel in Europe. They knew how to tip the waiters.

The waiters were so courteous with them as well, because they felt that the girls were well educated, and expressed such a refined mannerism. Furthermore, the girls also noticed that the chamber-maids were very courteous and friendly, however, they were concerned for the fact that they continued to stay in such an expensive hotel. One of the maids had the courage to establish a very serious conversation with them, after their sixth day stay. And then, she asked the young ladies we are just wondering whether you are just tourists, or you actually came to New York for another purpose?

Bipake's English was much better than Lunungi's. Lunungi was bashful and self-conscious to carry any conversation in English. Her big problem was to pronounce any word that has a "*TH* sound, example "*The*", she would sound "**Zeu**". And therefore, Bipake took the courage to explain to the chambermaid the reason why they actually wound up in that Hotel at that particular time. She said, "We really did not plan to stay here. It was in the emergency basis," she explained.

She continued our parents have close friends who work and live in this City. We are from the Congo. She stopped a while, and suddenly, she took out Zariap and Rolog's business cards from her purse to show them.

And then, both chamber-maids grasped that business card and began reading it. Their eyes grew wide-open as soon as they read "Precious Stones" business.

Further, they noticed the address on the card read, "Wall Street." The maids glanced at each other, and exclaimed, 'Oh, Wall Street! Are these individuals your families' friends?" They asked. The young ladies immediately replied in unison, "Yes, they are."

Another maid asked, "Have you ever met them in person?" Again, they answered in unison "Yes," we have. One continued, in fact, they have come to our country several times, she added. Finally Lunungi took a picture that was taken in Kinshasa, while they all had been having lunch on a Sunday at 1:00 p.m. in an exclusive restaurant in Kinshasa. In that picture, one can see, Mr. Zariap, Rolog and his wife, seated next to each other on the table, then, Mr. Bipake and his daughter *Bipake Ayele*, and Mr. Lunungi and his daughter **Lunungi Ebila** seated close to each other as well.

The Chambermaids were convinced that Zariap and Rolog were indeed close friends of the young ladies' parents, and that there was no doubt about it.

The chamber-maids became more curious, and then began inquiring further details. They continued to assess by asking diverse questions seeking to unravel the mysteries. Those maids were actually concerned, and therefore they continued to question the guests. "Did these people know that you were actually coming to New York City? But if they did, how is it then that they are letting you stay right at the airport hotel? This is far away from the city. There is absolutely nothing you can acquire around this location.

Your parents' business associates should have made better hotel accommodations at the midtown hotels where everything else is located; such as the shopping centers, modest restaurants, as well as the sightseeing. My colleagues and I have actually been discussing about this situation; and we had realized that it is the youth's nature to want to be close to where every activity is actually happening. And it is not going to happen here around this Kennedy airport. You will continue to observe nothing but all kinds of airplanes, takings off and landing. We are sure that this is not what you would actually want to see all days and all nights long. This is quite borrowing to newcomers; all us agreed with that statement. They were feeling sorry indeed for those young ladies.

Now, tell us what seems to be the story with Mr. Zariap and Mr. Rolog, few more chamber-maids joined the group. Bipake explained again, Zariap and Rolog have been the ones who stirred our fathers' desire to send us in this country in order to pursue our college education. They made this recommendation so that we can be able to acquire better education and especially to become proficient in English. This idea was beneficial to all of us, because both parties would have a better understanding of the business terminologies, as well as all the transactions involved.

Further, they told the maids about their initial plan, which had been to pursue their higher education in Brussels, because the school had awarded them scholarships. Furthermore, they also told them how Mr. Zariap and Rolog advised their parents regarding the excellent idea of allowing their daughters to come in this country, and acquire a broad school knowledge. They knew also that it would facilitate them to translate business matters from English into French, because their French was quite limited and rusty, so was our fathers English. Shortly after that,another hotel worker question, "weren't they aware of the day you were actually coming to New York?" Bipake right away replied, "Of course they have been aware since the last six months, this has been our regular subject with them.

In fact, a month prior to our arrival they have been reminded. Ten days prior to our departure, they knew we have arrived in Brussels. Furthermore, three days prior to our departure, we all have been conversing with each other. Finally the day we were supposed to leave Brussels, our respective fathers have spoken with both Zariap and Rolog. And, half an hour prior to taking off, Lunungi's father in fact all of us have also called them to get a confirmation from them whether or not they will pick us up, on Friday at 9:00 p.m. and yet all that time, they had assured our parents that all is in readiness, and that there was no need to be concerned.

In addition, Mr. Zariap and Rolog both had promised to assist us with accommodations and also to find a suitable School for us to register for ESL prior to taking AST or college entrance exam. We had landed in New York on Friday, at 9:00 p.m. and yet they were well aware of our itineraries, we cannot possibly comprehend the reason why they did not show up at the airport. We actually do not know anybody else here besides from Zariap and Rolog. The chamber-maids felt so badly to witness such an awful experience. This is disgrace said one of them. But how long do you plan to remain in this hotel, we are really concerned about that fact, because it is very expensive as you can see.

Bipake replied that we are actually trying to reach our parents and ask for advice unfortunately they had checked out of the hotel in Brussels. We are hoping that they go straight to Kinshasa, our home town. However, if they decide to go first to the East region of the country to attend another business meeting, we will wind up staying here for the next two weeks until we reached them. Until then, we are actually leaving everything in the hands of God for a suitable solution.

One the chambermaid got emotional and began to weep. She asked the girls, "Do you have any money that will last you until the next two weeks?" Bipake and Lunungi replied, "Yes we do have some money". All was actually provided, but not for a long stay in hotel. Three chambermaids came by again at the later time, and said to them: "We would like to advise you that if you know anybody that could actually help you to find a small apartment or even a room to rent, you will be better off paying a weekly or a monthly rent, rather than paying for a hotel room at a daily rate. That would be just too much, because your money would run out in a few days eventually. We actually feel sorry for you. Two young ladies in the foreign land!

Shortly, Bipake and Lunungi received a phone call from the gentleman from the airport. It was Mr. Pierrot Malsain. I said to Bipake who answered the phone that I just call to say hello, and to find out whether or not, you had been able to contact Zariap and Rolog during all that time. Both girls were extremely happy to hear from Pierrot Malsain, because he was the only individual they have met so far, and who appeared to be concerned about that issue. Bipake replied that they still had not been able to reach those gentlemen, unfortunately.

The girls seized the opportunity to ask Pierrot if he could stop by the hotel that day. Their intention was to request some help in terms of finding them a small vacant apartment or even a room they could rent on an emergency basis, rather than continuing to remain in such a costly hotel. Pierrot was kind enough to drop by the hotel during his break time. The maids advised Pierrot, if possible to try to find a small apartment or a room for the ladies to rent. Pierrot promised to inquire around, and to let them know as soon as he finds one.

Pierrot also asked the young ladies whether, or not they had made another attempt to reach Zariap and Rolog after the 7 days had been elapsed.

Bipake responded sadly, that they had re-tried several times, but still impossible to reach neither of them. So, Pierrot had made another attempt to call Zariap. Finally, Zariap answered the phone. Pierrot then told him, "I am calling on behalf of Bipake and Lunungi, and Zariap replied, "Oh, where are they by the way?" Pierrot said, "They are right here next to me as a matter of fact." Ziriap told Pierrot let me speak with one of them." Bipake was given the phone and said, "Hello Mr. Zariap!"

Zariap asked her where you are staying at. Bipake replied that we are at the International hotel by Kennedy airport. Zariap replied "I know it that is actually a very good hotel. I would like the gentleman to bring you here in my Wall Street office. Actually let me just speak with him." Bipake passed the phone to Pierrot. Zariap told Pierrot can you bring the ladies to my office tomorrow at 11:00 a.m.? Pierrot accepted. Zariap dictated his Wall Street address to Pierrot. And the next day, Pierrot took a day off from his job, and escorted the young ladies to meet Mr. Zariap in Wall Street via a yellow cab, which took them from International airport hotel to Wall Street, at their own expense. Zariap's office was located on the 27th floor, whereas Rolog's was located on the 25th floor in the same building.

Pierrot Escorted Bipake and Lunungi to Meet with Mr. Zariap and Rolog

As soon as they had arrived in the building, the security guards had already been notified of their arrival, and immediately, buzzed Zariap's office to signal their arrival. Pierrot and both young ladies took the elevator, and got off on the 27th floor. It was amazing to notice that Zariap's office was composed of three tiny little offices; one must pass the first, then the second, and then, the third secluded little office where Zariap was actually confined. Bipake reported that Zariap was seated below a huge device used to cut and polished those precious stones.

Zariap greeted the young ladies. After conversing with them for about five minutes, he then picked up his phone and called Mr. Rolog whose office was two flights below. He asked him to come up immediately to his office. As soon as he perceived the young ladies, Rolog appeared iced cold to them. He greeted them as though he had never previously had any close association with those girls.

And yet, while in the Congo, he was known to be the most humorous gentleman they have ever known, especially at the dinner table.

Generally, both Zariap and Rolog appeared less eager while in New York than while they had always been in the Congo. Zariap acted a little bit diplomatically about it. Whereas Rolog did not have such an expertise, one could tell that he was not happy at all to see Bipake and Lunungi in New York. Nevertheless, women are very receptive. They had caught those negative vibrations in the air somehow. It was appalling indeed to them. However, Pierrot Malsain, their new friend was such a comfort to them. Physically, he was viewed as though he were their guardian Angel or a gift from God.

In fact, Miss Bipake had in her possession a letter size envelope, which was addressed to Mr. Rolog. In effect, and inside that envelope was Mr. Rolog's bounced check, which he had made payable to Mr. Bipake while he was in Kinshasa. The check was returned to Congo while Mr. Rolog was back to New York. The check was stamped "NSF". It was precisely marked, "Non Sufficient Funds." In addition, it was stamped, "This Account had already been closed." As soon as Mr. Rolog received that envelope, he opened it right there and then.

However, as soon as he had noticed his wrong deeds, he frowned suddenly. Of course, Rolog became uncomfortable to realize such an awful action.

Shortly afterwards, he left Mr. Zariap's office immediately, and that without bidding the guests goodbye. All he said to Zariad was, "I must get going, for I have a lot to do." Then, he suddenly disappeared from the scene.

Apparently, in order to cover up that shameful scenario, Mr. Zariap told Pierrot, "here is the five dollar bill ($5.00) you can take the young ladies out; show them downtown. He grinned a little, and added, "They have money believe me, they will add to what I have just given you, if they want to see a show or anything they wish; in fact their parents are well to do in their country, " He told Pierrot, giggling. Subsequently, Pierrot asked to use the man's room, but his intension was to pull himself away, and be able to listen what Zariap had to tell the girls at his absence. Surely, as soon as Pierrot left the group, Zariap questioned the girls.

"Who is that young man? Where did you meet him?" They replied that they met him at the airport, and he has been the one who has been helping us all along to reach you. He is the one also who made hotel accommodations for us" Mr. Zariap acted suspicious, he told the girls, but here in this city, you must be very careful, because guys are very quick to harm girls O.k?" Pierrot had heard everything, but did not comment when he came back from the man's room.

However, on their way back, Pierrot told the girls that as I have
indicated previously, I am in the Service, we are taught to be
ready at a moment notice. Therefore we are always alert.
Zariap had no idea I was listening to every word he was telling
you.

When Zariap was getting ready to dismiss the guests,
Bipake raised a question regarding accommodations and the
School assistance which they had promised them while they
were in the Congo. Zariap right away, frowned and said,
"Well, ladies, I regret to inform you that our business deal with
your families is actually off. You have a return ticket home,
you might as well return home after few days stay, if you so
desire. The girls were actually shocked to hear such a negative
statement from Zariap.

Finally, the girls asked more details regarding the
reason why the business deal had to actually fail? Zariap
replied that because no agreement was actually reached with
their prospective partners in regard to the distribution of the
revenue. He said that we actually were asking 75%, because
we have travel expenses to cover, and we were offering them
25%, because they do not have any travel expenses.

Nevertheless, they disagreed bluntly with our ideas. Further, they raised the question of overhead expenses, which they have to cover. So they feel that such distribution appears unfair to them however we had tried to present it. In fact, we attempted to convince them that, it does not matter even though they will have to pay the overhead expense. Due to the fact that they are dealing with a cheap labor, the overhead expenses, we believe, would actually be minimum, probably 2% or even less.

The partners continued, regardless to our clear explanations, Mr. Bipake and his partner Lunungi would not sign our agreement. They felt that our suggestions were nothing but a fallacy, as far as their perception was concerned. No business deal can be obtained and sustained under such circumstance and retribution. There is no use to get into any business deal that would yield a negative profit. Those were their answers to our suggestions. We felt that they were very pessimistic; probably their Belgian partners had a lot to do with that. In addition, your parents gave us the impression that we probably were attempting to cheat them. So we figured, if that the way they felt about our business deal, then we might as well forget about the entire business deal in the Congo.

We will actually seek another African country where we can get a better deal. Mr. Zariap concluded; and turning his head left and right. He finally shrugged.

Miss Bipake and Lunungi, glanced at each other, and Bipake repeated, "Mr. Zariap you indicated that the reason you business deal did not work out was due to the fact that you were requesting a distribution of 75%, because of your travel expenses, and you were offering our fathers 25%, because the overhead is not significant, and also because they do not need to travel to your country? Oh, thank you for explaining, we understand now why you could not reach an agreement if that was how the distribution of revenue was supposed to be among you. Zariap replied, "yes, that was the main reason. We do not want to make a negative profit either, you see. We believe that Mr. Bipake had made a big error by employing Belgians. We think that they had badmouthed us that could be the reason why our business transactions were unsuccessful.

Furthermore, Mr. Zariap said to them, "So, you girls just be informed that we are not going to be able to assist you, as we had previous thought. If you wish however, instead of desiring to study here, you should rather go back to Europe where you had initially planned to go.

In fact, it would also be better for your parents to see you on a regular basis, whenever they come to attend business meeting with their Belgian partners, who happen to be so privileged.

The young ladies were eventually disappointed and felt helpless. As they were about to bid them goodbye, Zariap added, unfortunately we cannot help you, but since your visa is not expired yet you should report to your Embassy so they may be aware of your presence in this country. That is why the Embassies are created around the world, besides from establishing diplomatic relations between countries, they also have the obligation to render service to their own fellow citizens who are in need in the foreign land. The ladies thanked Mr. Zariap for clarifying the entire situation about their relationship, and then, they departed from his office. In their way back to hotel, Pierrot said to the girls, "I am so grateful that I had accompanied you, because I now understand almost all the details regarding your situation. He added, but that was a weird business deal which he was actually defending. Pierrot had a good sense of humor. He made a joke out of it. "I will receive 75% and you have to accept 25%! What a great business deal!" Pierrot added.

Bipake felt obligated to relate his father earliest experience, while he was employed by a Belgian's enterprise in the Congo. She said, "Pierrot, you see, my father underwent a higher degree of injustice as an employee. That is why he actually decided to become self-employer. And from that negative experience, he had become adamant when it comes to business transactions. He would not tolerate any unfair deal." Pierrot interrupted, is it true what Zariap had voiced? Do you your parents really have a lot of money, or he was just mocking them?" Bipake replied, Pierrot as I have just indicated, "my father did not start rich in his life. He had worked extremely hard in the Belgian's enterprise. He exhibited strength and ability to do his work, as a result, he was given the responsibility to train new employees, whom his boss used to hire. The employer used to hire them just because they were from his home town in Belgium, and yet, he knew they were not qualified, but out of pity, he knew they needed to make a living.

The boss would at the same time play as a role of a double agent; in front of my father, he would praise his work, and would bad mouthed his less educated countrymen, who wrote French poorly.

Initially, he used to beg my father to begin training them from scratch, and to be very patient with them, because most of them have just a minimum level of education from their country and had never acquired any office experience in their lives, whatsoever from home. Behind my father's back, the boss would tell his countrymen, let him train you really good. You will actually become his supervisors after this training period, and will be receiving a very high salary. He gets paid close to nothing, laughter!

Ultimately few months afterwards, those individuals would eventually become my father's superiors. They would begin bossing him around, and addressing him inappropriately. In addition, their salaries would be much higher than his. In fact, they would get paid double portions, one part in their country's currency, for their savings purpose, and another portion would be in Congolese currency for their local expenses. And yet, those individuals performed poorly; incapable of writing a report or even a simple correct paragraph in French, which is their native language. Consequently, the boss would always send their reports to my father in order to check their spelling and grammar, prior to presenting it at the meeting.

In the light of this, his boss would be stern in terms of adjusting my father's salary. In effect, he would avoid discussing any salary or promotion issues, regardless to the fact that my father was a married man, with three children to nurture; the boss was just unsympathetic. When my father's small and old car was broken, he was unable to repair it, because he had no money to have it repaired. Consequently, he had to sell it very cheap; and replaced it with a bike.

When I was in the fourth grade, my father began taking me to school on a bike, because he could not afford to renew my bus subscription. He drove my mother to the clinic on a bike as well. You see, my father did not start rich. He was so depressed with such an injustice. Thank God, he gave obedience to his friend, who began to invite him to his church. He was finally taught how to renew his mind and receive God's unconditional love and justice. That was the turning point of his life. God gave him the strength to resign from that job, and began a small traditional furniture business, selling tiny small chairs

(Ebonga), Fufu Rod, African Sculptures, and traditional musical instrument (**Mpuita, Mizakisa**, etc..). His grandmother was a pottery maker from his village. He sold potteries as well. Certainly, the hand of God was upon that small business.

Ultimately, his business grew enormously. That was how he gathered enough money to get into precious stones business. Later on, he became partner with Mr. Lunungi." Miss Lunungi also told her father earlier miseries. "My father also did not start rich in his life. His father (my grandfather) was a fisherman in Equator Area. My father used to sell fishes, plantains, and fresh coffee. He used to buy some fishes from Lake Tanganyika as well, whenever he went to small city of Kalemie. This was how he got the money to start serious business, and became partners with Mr. Bipake. They have been working harmoniously together ever since that time. That is why Zariap and Rolog found them with the big Cadillacs and huge homes; they endeavored to earn what they have," Lunungi added. Pierrot was interested in hearing this narrative. He said, "I do not actually blame your parents for not signing such an unfair contract. Don't be concerned, if your parents can help finance your college education, you will no longer need them."

Besides, they were only going to help us find a good school and arrange for housing accommodations at our own expenses," Bipake added. "I will bring you to School and you will be on your way. I ensure to find an apartment for you, prior to my return, Pierrot assured them. However, be careful, do not let anyone here know that your parents have a lot of money, it is very dangerous, Zariap should not have divulged such private information for your security. And yet, he knows it better," Pierrot said. Both girls responded, "We also felt badly about it.

On one hand, he's advising us to be careful with guys in this city, they are too quick; and on the other hand, he is revealing our fathers' private information, Lunungi added.Bipake and Lunungi's dismay was so great. Naturally, it was depressing because Zariap and Rolog were the ones who had actually recommended the girls' families to send their daughters abroad in order to acquire college education in New York, instead of letting them go and pursue their higher education in Europe. Zariap and Rolog could have advised the girls and their respective fathers to let they girls remain in Brussels, due to the fact that the business deal was no longer being considered. Nevertheless, they failed to notify the girls and their parents over the phone. Consequently, the young ladies followed their previous itineraries, and eventually came and experienced diverse challenges in New York City. Nevertheless, they overcame them all.

However, few days later Pierrot was able to find them a one bedroom apartment in Brooklyn. That apartment had two bed rooms and a Kitchen, and it also had one main bath room and a shower room. There was already one tenant in that apartment; she was renting one of the rooms. She was a middle age lady, and appeared very quiet by nature. She stated that her husband stayed back home in Haiti with her son. She actually came in this country to seek for employment. She was a factory worker and was saving her money diligently, so that she could bring her spouse and her son in this country, she told them.

The young ladies were so grateful to Pierrot, for taking the initiatives of assisting them to the point where they could find an apartment to rent. At last they were able to check out of the International hotel, and then, move in an apartment. They found it very economical to pay a monthly rent, which cost them almost close to nothing, compared to paying hotel daily rate. The only thing the girls regretted a little bit was the fact that they had lost the privilege of having a room service at the hotel, as well as having the beds fixed by the chambermaids.

They have a roof over their head at least for the time being, although it was in old four-story building. They had to start from scratch, because they were lacking cooking utensils

as well as bed linen, and quilts. Lunungi decided to go and buy
them in the nearby stores. Lunungi realized that she might
have difficulties expressing herself in terms of asking the items
needed, so prior to going to store, she ensured to carry with her
a very small French-English dictionary in her hand. As soon as
she got near the store, about few steps away, she stopped in the
corner to look up the words (sheet, blanket and quilt). While
she was busy looking up the words, one gentleman approached
her, and offered to help her. She asked him where she could
buy the bed linen and cooking utensils. The gentleman realized
that she was a newcomer in the community. He directed her
towards the right store; however he kept on following her, and
extended his hand to ask for money.

Lunungi opened her purse innocently, and had noticed
that the ten dollars bill was on the top of the other small
denominations which she had in her purse. As soon as the
gentleman saw the bill, he got all excited, and suddenly, he
snatched the ten dollar bill from her purse quickly, and then ran
away as fast as he could towards an opposite direction.
Lunungi stood there watching him as he vanished in the crowd.
Lunungi said to herself, so the gentleman was actually a thief.
She concluded that this was another negative experience in this
City. However, she purchased all the items needed. The
salespeople were honest and courteous.

The ladies were so grateful to Pierrot for having rendered them such a great service, and in return, in order to show their appreciation to him, each one of them gave him one hundred dollar bill in order to thank him for all his endeavors. Pierrot was so touched to notice that sign of gratitude, which came from the bottom of the the girls' hearts.

Pierrot knew that he was scheduled to resume his Service activities abroad. Therefore, he made sure to find a school for his friends, and help them with registration prior to his departure. Finally the time came for Pierrot to say goodbye to Bipake and Lunungi. Lunungi, reported, that "it was a sad moment indeed. Although they knew Pierrot for a short duration, because he endeavored in helping them resolve most of their problems, the young ladies viewed him as if he were one of their family members, or a Déjà Vu.

They hated to see him go away. Bipake said, "Bidding Pierrot goodbye was such heartbreaking experience. We felt helpless, Lunungi and I, because around Pierrot, we felt very confident, being that he was bilingual; every time, he would translate and explain things with which we were not familiar. There was no other closer person around us. The ladies were indeed touched to see Pierrot go away, with no hope of seeing him again. They could not help weeping, because he had become like a big brother to them. They viewed him sometimes, as an Angel in the flesh, who had been placed at the Airport to welcome them to New York City, and render them the service which Mr. Zariap and Rolog had failed to accomplish. Besides, he exemplified a high degree of honesty in handling their money.

While they were staying in the apartment with their Haitian roommate, they had noticed however that she hardly spent time in the living room. She was spending most of her time in her bedroom rather than in the living room, but she appeared to be kind to the young ladies, in her own way.

One day however, Bipake was sitting in the living room and the roommate was standing while she was relating a short incident which had just occurred in that building. Bipake had seized that opportunity and asked her to be seated next to them, instead of continuing the conversation while standing. The roommate alluded to her landlord appearance.

Well, usually he gets in here spontaneously, because he has the key to this apartment. He would actually be concerned to see me sitting in the living room. Bipake continued, so what will happen if he sees you in the seated position? Hearing this question, the neighbor felt then obligated to open up, and explained that, actually, prior to your moving in here, she had been advised by the landlord that he was going to charge the new tenants more than she was being charged. And therefore, he wanted the newcomers to feel that they were actually renting a one bedroom apartment, and not just a room. He wanted their rent to reflect the size of the entire apartment. She continued, the landlord is aware that you people, coming from Africa have more money than I do, the roommate concluded, with a smile.

The Landlord Advised the Young Ladies to Meet the Congolese Consul General

One day however, the landlord stopped by and started to carry on a long conversation with the young ladies, and suddenly he asked the girls, by the way since you have arrived in New York City have been to your Consulate? They replied that not yet. He continued, well I think you real should go and introduce yourself to your Consulate it is important because if you ever needed help on governmental level your Consulate can actually help you. So, Bipake and Lunungi thought it was a very good advice. So, they had inquired the neighbors how to get to the Congolese Consulate. The neighbors were kind enough to find them the Consulate phone number. They decided to call the Congolese Consulate in order to make an appointment. They were given an appointment to meet the

Consul. They were asked to bring with them their Congolese passports in order to confirm their identities.

Eventually, they did follow the instructions, and went to the Congolese Consulate which was located on the Second Avenue in Manhattan. Upon arriving at the Consulate, they had introduced themselves to the receptionist, and requested to see the Consul General.

Suddenly, the Deputy Consul came to the reception area in order to greet the girls. He said to them, "Unfortunately the Consulate General is absent at the moment. He is attending a meeting at the United Nations." So he ask them to present their Congolese passports in order to verify their Congolese citizenship, and they did. He looked to see whether or not their visas were expired; fortunately their visas were still valid but were going to be expired within two months. He asked them diplomatically, how can we help you? So, the ladies seized the opportunity to inquire about the appropriate procedure of renewing their visas when they will finally expire.

The deputy Consul started to pepper young ladies with questions, "how did you actually come here in this country?" They told him their little story with Zariap and Rolog who were supposed to help them for accommodations and the school matters. Things did not work out as it had been planned.

So they also confirmed that currently they were left on their own trying to do everything they can in order to start college.

Diplomats' Reaction against the Young Ladies' Visit

The deputy Consul was not sympathetic at all but acted diplomatically, saying to them well, I will relate your message to the Consul General and whatever he replies you will be notified. In the meantime he asked the address where they were staying and the phone number where they could have been reached, and so they did give their address and neighbor's phone number because they did not have their own phone available yet at that time. He took the whole situation in the negative way.

He elaborated a negative report about the girls without any further investigation. He also informed every diplomat in the office, saying that I feel suspicious about those two girls; and how can anyone explain the fact that these young ladies just arrived in this country no long ago, just few weeks ago and yet they have already renting an one bedroom apartment in Brooklyn? This is a very serious matter indeed. He insisted that everyone should be cautious to deal with them. They do not appear to be normal people. They are probably up to something maybe to check on us, and no matter what kind of help they require, we are not going to bend in helping them, the deputy consul advised everyone in the office. They made all kind of comments on their appearance. They said, "Look at those expensive outfits each one of them is wearing!". Another one said, "And did you notice all those expensive jewelries and watches they are wearing?" Every word that was spoken expressed nothing, but a spirit of extreme dislike towards the girls.

However, because their address and phone number were made available to every diplomat in the office, and they were about eight diplomats altogether at that time; then six got together, and decided "we are going to abuse these two girls", so they thought. Therefore, they then began calling them two diplomats at a time, in order to woo them. However at every attempt, the girls were stern and firmed and they would simply reply to them that "unfortunately, we are very busy right now trying to get our school matters straight up.

Therefore, we cannot start with any other thing besides from our primary duty in this country which is our School matters." Regardless to those counselors' insistence, all the diplomats met with resistance from the young ladies. They actually failed utterly.

Their evil intent could not have manifested. The girls were very wise; they concluded, number one, all of those men were married with children, and number two, based on their appearance, all those men could have never been able to approach them if they had been in their own country, because they were daughters of wealthy businessmen. And therefore, they would have never dared to do it.

Due to the fact that their destructive plan had failed them utterly, as a result, they had become very furious and hateful towards the girls; and they had made it a very serious case. Each of them would go and urge the Deputy Consul to write an awful report concerning these two girls, they would tell him, "See if we can get them deported back to the Congo; and who they think they are? Counselors were saying to each other, those girls are really setting themselves way too high.

It was reported that one of them was so angry and said, "We probably appeared to those queens as though, we are unworthy to take them out." Further another counselor commented saying, "Take notice of this, based on their French diction they sound as though they might have studied in Paris from their childhood; even the Ambassador's secretary who is the French born from Marseilles had noticed as well," the diplomat concluded. Another counselor answered, so what even if their parents are well to do. We do not have to be intimidated by them. We have been living in this country longer than they do. They have just arrived here; and we can scare the hell out of them, until to the point to get them to return on their own, another counselor added. The gentlemen's egos had been really hurt. They were therefore frustrated, due to the fact that they were turned down, and they decided to revenge.

Because Deputy Consult initially had some degree of resentment against the girls as well, he then became charged with the comments from colleagues against the girls. Therefore he had decided to call a meeting in order to caution all the counselors, he said, "this is really a strange thing when you stop to think, since we had been in this office we had never ever seen this case before."

Two High School graduates of that age to come in this country by themselves, can anyone explain the fact that these young ladies have just arrived in New York, and in few weeks, they are settled in a one bedroom apartment in Brooklyn, and who is paying for their rent? How in the world can this be possible? They are not ordinaries people. All the diplomats agreed with this suspicious hypothesis. One of them said, this is just weir and strange indeed, so beware people! He warned them. We are not going to assist them. They probably are sent to check on us. We have never seen young ladies of their age from our country to come this far here on their own, and get settled right away in one of the well known borough. This is not funny, he told everybody in the office. We should get American authority involved and deport them back

Deputy Consul's Meeting with Consul General

So, the Deputy Consul was urged to write a memorandum to the Consul General addressing everyone's complaint against the girls. Their intention was to make the Consul General to seize the US immigration's Officials so that they can start a deportation action against those two girls. The Consul General read the memo, and in the last sentence it read, His Excellency, please use all your authority to convince the Immigration's officers to deport these two girls immediately because they appear to be trouble makers. All the counselors were so excited about the outcome of this situation. They could not wait to see the Consul General reaction in this matter.

However, the Consul General told his Deputy that prior to seizing the US Immigration's officers I would like you to bring me the photocopies of Bipake and Lunungi's passports in order to verify the validity of their US visas. Deputy Consul called the receptionist and ordered her to bring the copies of the

ladies' passports. When the Consul General had examined
their passports, he realized that their tourists' visas were still
valid for eight more weeks.

He reminded his Deputy that, "we must bear in mind
that prior to seizing US Immigration's officers being an
Ambassador, the case which I present should be valid. Bear in
mind the government officials are well qualified so whichever
case presented to them would be examined carefully.
Questions would be asked prior to considering your allegations.
I do now wish to appear as an unwise Ambassador. You should
also remember that as long as an individual's visa is still valid,
that person is considered to be legally in that foreign land; and
he or she cannot be termed an illegal alien.

The Consul general decided to push away all the copies
as well as the deputy Consul's report included the memo that
was attached to them back to him. Finally, the deputy consul
was asked "Are you certain that all of you can come out with
another valid excuse, which would make sense to the
Immigrations' Officials? He continued, bear in mind that the
Immigration Officials are well trained individuals in terms of
examining each allegation. They do not act as those in the
Third world countries would, and therefore they wouldn't just
deport a tourist because we just wish it to be so. It has to be a

legitimate reason. Prior to taking such action, they must make an assessment and evaluation of the case. I would not want to be taken as a fool. Again, remember, we are not in the Third world countries here.

He therefore ordered the Deputy Consul to go and speak with the other diplomats, and when you actually find a valid excuse, you then can reiterate your request, until then, I do not want to have anything to do with those famous young ladies. As far as I am concerned, that isn't the job I have been hired to do here is this office. He said it firmly. Apparently, the diplomat was embarrassed, and gathered all his reports; finally he walked out of his boss's office, disgracefully.

CHAPTER III

Meeting Maseko and Missionaries at the Airport

Few days later, Bipake and Lunungi received a phone call from Seattle. It was Lunungi's family friend called Miriam Maseko. Their families lived in the same borough, in fact few blocks from each other. But Maseko being four year older than Lunungi, had graduated four years earlier from the same High School, and had been privileged of obtaining a scholarship from her parents' church, which had brought her to pursue her

college education to Seattle, Washington State. Maseko were
able to establish the communication. She had called to inform
Lunungi that she had recently been in touch with her family
inthe Congo and that her father had spoken with Mr. Lunungi.
The both figured that it was indeed necessary that we establish
close contact while we are in the United State. At the same
time, Maseko informed Lunungi that she will be passing
through New York City within a week, because she had to
travel to Congo for family emergency, her dear mother was
not well, and that she had requested to see her, should anything
happen to her.

Maseko begged Lunungi to do the best she could in
meeting her at Kennedy airport. Bipake knew Maseko as well,
because her Sister Madiya had graduated from the same High
School during the same year. Maseko notified Lunungi and
Bipake of her itineraries. Her flight from Kennedy's airport
was scheduled to depart at 11:00 p.m. and she was to arrive
from Seattle at 6:00 p.m. Lunungi and Bipake were ready to
meet her at the airport that evening, and in addition, they also
had felt that the opportunity was appropriate to send
correspondence to their respective families.

Apparently, Lunungi and Bipake had been under the
impression that Miriam Maseko would be sitting by herself at

the airport since she did not know anyone else in New York
City, except the two girls. Howeve, when they had arrived at
the area where she was sitting, all of a sudden they had noticed
an elderly couple next to her talking closely with her. As soon
as Miriam Maseko spotted Lunungi and Bipake, she stood up
quickly, and hugged each of them. She then introduced each
one to the couple who were still seated.

Maseko Introduce Missionaries, Mr. and Mrs. Brown to Her Friends

She continued, please meet Mr. and Mr. Brown, they
were missionaries in the Congo for so many years. All of a
sudden, Mrs. and Mr. Brown, stood up eagerly, and shook
hands, and then, hugged them. They added, how glad they were
to meet the Congolese people once again. Mrs. Brown
continued, "Oh you have no idea how much we really miss our
Congolese friends!" Shortly after that, all of them sat down.
Mrs. Brown was slim and taller than her husband, who
appeared stout about six inches shorter, but she was outspoken,
she continued. We felt at home in Congo. The Congolese
people are such warm people, and we had enjoyed having them
as our closest friends during all our stay in that country.

Thank God, we have kept in touch with Maseko's families. This is what has made it possible to meet Maseko today. It is unfortunate that Maseko has to travel in a family emergency. Both husband and wife were so eager to meet Bipake and Lunungi. They thanked Maseko for making sure to invite them at the airport, which had allowed the couple to meet with them. Right then, the couple requested to have their address and phone number where they could be easily reached. Further, the couple promised to invite them over their home in Connecticut, shortly after that brief encounter.

The couple appeared so inquisitive, and they had made certain to get all the necessary details about the young ladies' presence in this country. During all that time, the couple could not stop asking one question after another in the attempt to explore the truth regarding their arrival in this country. The following were the type of questions the couple asked them: "Did you come here on scholarship? Who sponsored you here? How did you find an apartment in Brooklyn? Who had helped you to find that apartment? How much is your rent? Who is paying for that rent?

Apparently, Bipake and Lunungi were so naïve in front of that couple. They had trusted them with all their hearts due to the fact that they were missionaries, and also for the fact that they had lived in their country for several years. And therefore, they felt somewhat obligated to answer all their questions without any reservation. After jotting down all the necessary information they needed regarding the young ladies, the couple decided to drive back to Connecticut because it started getting very late, also for the fact that Maseko's flight had to take off in two more hours. They bade Maseko goodbye and wished her nice trip to Congo.

Mr. Brown reminded Maseko "Do not forget to take the bag of clothing we have brought for you to take to Congo and share them among our friends. After hugging Maseko, they turned and reminded Bipake and Lunungi, "We will invite you at our home in the near future." Bipake and Lunungi felt so uplifted to meet such a wonderful couple, who had such a wonderful experience in their country. They also felt that the couple's invitation would be gladly accepted whenever they would decide to invite them at their home, in Connecticut.

Because Maseko's flight was scheduled to take off at 11:00 p.m. Bipake and Lunungi had to depart due to the fact that they had to attend school the next morning, around 10:15 they decided to bid their friend goodbye. However, prior to departing, Maseko said to them: "I have two big pieces of luggage and one big hand bag to carry.

The couple had just handed me a bag full of shift clothing to bring to my mother and other ladies. Maseko, said to Lunungi and Bipake, I am going to open this bag to see whether or not it is worthy carrying the raggedy clothing to people who would never wear them, at this point in time. Maseko opened the bag in front of her friends, and began to lift one piece at a time. It was amazing to notice how worn out those clothes appeared! They were faded and colorless.

Maseko and her friends looked at each other, and then shook their heads. Maseko, explained, well, we have to bear in mind that this couple had left the country since 1958. They still perceive things the same way they had actually been years ago. They pitied them, because they had not had another opportunity to travel back to Congo and view the change.

They girls understood that they actually meant well, however no body would ever wear those obsolete items. For that that reason, Maseko asked Bipake and Lunungi to take that bag with them, and see if there would be anybody in the building who might want them. Initially, they had been very reluctant to drag that bag with them, but they decided to take it anyway, and showed it to their roommate. Unfortunately, nobody wanted them in the building, as a results they were discarded.

Mrs. and Mrs. Brown Conduct a Research at the Congolese Consulate

Shortly after their exciting meeting at the airport, the couple could not digest to see two Congolese, 18 year old female, High School graduate traveling alone in such a big city of New York. They had just refused to accept their narrative, and all the details involved in it. The couple was so inquisitive apparently, and they needed to explore more about Bipake and Lunungi. Therefore, they decided to drive to the Congolese Consulate in Manhattan, just to

satisfy their curiosity. As soon as they arrived in the office, they requested to meet with the Consul General immediately. Unfortunately, they were told, "His Excellence Ambassador is not available at this time. He is actually attending a very important meeting the United Nations Building. Then, the receptionist buzzed deputy Consul to speak with the couple. He came to greet them and asked them, "How can I help you?" They replied that we needed to talk to the Consul General privately. He told them that at his absence, it is I who assume the office responsibilities. So he invited them in his office and closed the door behind them in order to listen to concerns.

Mrs. Brown the outspoken person told him, "We have a concern to address to you as the Representative of Congo. We know the Congolese people very well, because we had lived and worked in your country for so many years. We left your country in 1958 and we had been there since 1941. As far as we are concerned the students of their ages can only come to study in this country when we, missionaries sponsor them. We are indeed shocked and amazed to hear their story. It just does not seem to be real. Do you know anything about their coming here in this country?

The deputy consul, who was already resentful towards the girls, was charged with that inquiry; and he replied to them that we all are wondering about this seeming issue. However, it is better that you came to bring your concern about this situation. Together, your efforts and ours will do something ultimately, and we will come out with an adequate solution. The deputy consul took the information from that couple, and promise to pass into the Consul General, and also to share the concern with the rest of the diplomatic corps. And after hearing the missionaries' concerns, everyone in the office became over excited. They knew that they have a serious case against Bipake and Lunungi. Ultimately, they will have an unwanted surprise, they said to themselves.

Deputy Consul and diplomats found an Alibi to Harass the Girls.

Based on that spirit of resentment and hatred, all the counselors in the office had repeatedly stirred up the Deputy Consul to write another negative report about the girls, and addressed it once more to the Consul General. All the diplomats were so excited with Mr. and Mrs. Browns' concerns about those young ladies' presence here, in New York City. So, he elaborated every negative aspect which would cause the Consul General to actually get annoyed with the girls, and especially to take an immediate legal action against them, although without any apparent reason.

The report was actually to convince him that those girls were probably sent to cause us trouble. He wrote, "We do not actually know how in the world they came in this country. In addition, they have the audacity to impose us to help them to renew their US expired visas. Is that our duty in this office to take care of their US visas? The deputy consul wanted actually to make sure that the Consul General will not change his mind in acknowledging those two young ladies.

In fact, the Consul General knew nothing else about the young ladies, except all the negative aspects created against them, and transmitted to him by his peers. The deputy Consult added in his report the following statement,"Even Mr. and Mrs. Brown, who had been missionaries in the Congo from 1941-1958, they too, agreed with us. We are not the only ones who are concerned about this issue. The missionaries are urging us to actually find a good reason of deporting them back to Congo.

They said that they actually find it very suspicious indeed to notice two young ladies in such a huge city alone. We noticed that they appear well dressed with expensive jewelries and watches, which the rest of us cannot afford. Usually, the church is the one who supposed to sponsor all the African students in this country. Basically, the missionaries had made their assessment by asking them whether or not they are being sponsored by any particular church or organization. But, they had declined! Missionaries had said that they cannot digest this fact, it is just enormous! And therefore, all of us should find out the truth about these two young ladies, and everyone should do their part, in order to come out with some physical evidence.

The missionaries' visit to the Consulate had made such a negative impact around the office. The diplomatic corps felt that because Mr. and Mrs. Brown were missionaries and also

American citizens, they would have enough power to just seize the Immigration Department and arrange for deportation without any delays or any judgment.

However, neither missionaries nor diplomatic corps knew that the ladies were already enrolled in an accredited school where they were taking English course. During that time, the School had already explained to the students that their B-1 visas were being processed to F-1 status. And therefore, the young ladies were just calmed, because they knew that they were in good standing with the laws of the country.

The Consul General's Decision Based on the Negative Report against the Girls

Having read that negative report, the Consul General flared, and he was actually fuming. Suddenly, he ordered the Deputy Consul to delegate the Second counselor to immediately get in touch with those young ladies in order to reprimand and eventually to intimidate them! So Mr. Mutoto, the Second Counselor, was designated to call Bipake and Lunungi in order to relate the Consul General's message. My name is counselor Mutoto; I am calling in the behalf of the Consul General. You should bear in mind that, "

The Consul General has nothing to do with both of you. In whichever manner, you had come in this country, he actually does not want to get involved or be disturbed by you.

Further, he said to inform you that, "He does not even want to meet you, and you are no longer allow to access the Consulate office in the attempt to request any sort of assistance. Our office is actually open to serve the American people only, that means, businessmen and tourists, and not for you to come in and create a chaos. I wish to reiterate that you ladies are no longer permitted to set your foot, at the Consulate again in order to cause any disorder among the diplomatic corps. Remember however that if you do come again at the Consulate, The Consulate General would have to seize the American authority, and have you deported immediately without any judgment.

Mr. Mutoto continued, as a matter of fact, we do not know exactly how and why you are here in New York City, anyway!" We don't care and we do not even want to know it. It is none of our business to get involved with your visas issues. If your visas have been expired, then you should just get your return ticket, and go right back home without disturbing the Consul General.

We are very busy with diplomatic matters at the United Nations, and we do not have time to waste handling Congolese tourists' confusions."

In addition, Mr. Mutoto continued, out of curiosity, "May I ask who ever had sent you here? Nevertheless, whoever that person is, let that individual handle your mess. Our office doesn't want to see you ever again. Every one of us assumes that you are not here to cause us trouble. We estimate that that is not your intention otherwise, we would dismiss you here, and direct you somewhere else!" The counselor sounded very unpleasant to listen to. He added, "Miss, did you get the Consul General's official message? Bipake could not comprehend the cause of this whole issue.

She was eventually so shocked that she could hardly find any proper word to pronounce at that particular moment. Because she was well educated, and knew that a Consulate office is supposed to be an Extension of a citizen's government in a Foreign Land. So, she wondered, was the Congolese Consulate assuming different functions in the Foreign Land or just the diplomatic corps lack any legal training in order to occupy the positions of trust? Bipake and Lunungi could not quite comprehend the origin of this issue.

And could not understand why people had created something out of nothing? Where was that hatred coming from? Was it out of jealousy?

Lunungi had been observing Bipake's body language during the entire conversation with the diplomat. At the end of the conversation, Bipake turned to Lunungi, help her head, and shook her heard slowly. And then she began to explain the content of the conversation to Lunungi. She said, "My dear, this is an amazing situation. The man, who had just called, is a diplomat, a Second Counselor at the Congolese Consulate.

He said he had been delegated by the Consul General in order to tell us that "The Consulate is not designed to handle Congolese tourists' confusions. Further, the Consul General said, "He does not want to see us at the Consulate building ever again." He also said that, we should bear in mind that it is not his responsibility to actually advise us regarding the change of our US visas or a status.

He also made it clear, according to the counselor that "Whoever who had taken the responsibilities to sent us here, let him or her take the responsibilities to handle our mess. It should not actually be him or his counselors to do so." Bipake continued, Lungungi, Mr. Mutoto so called, sounded really mean and gross. Both of them could not quite understand the cause of all that hostility toward them.   They were just surprised and depressed to notice that even their own countrymen had to act cunningly toward them. The young ladies looked at each other, and said to each other, "we had thought that the Consulate or the Embassy are the extensions of a Country in a foreign land, if this is not so but what are their functions?" They were busy seeking the cause of those people's aggressiveness, and they just could not pinpoint it.

In the meantime, the young ladies began to recall what they had noticed while they were sitting at the reception area in the Consulate office. They diplomats started to parade back and forth. At that time, they had no slightest idea in regard to diplomats' peculiar behaviors and movement. Probably, it was the office's norms or just a daily routine that forced employees to move from one office to another, in a very short interval, the young ladies had thought. Ultimately, they realized that the diplomats' parade constant movement was actually to allow employees to just take a close look of the young ladies, who were seated at the waiting area. Eventually, the young ladies' presence made everyone excited. They wondered who they actually were, and why they had come.

The young ladies ultimately regretted for having listened to their first landlord's advice. They had wished they did not have to travel all the way from Brooklyn to Manhattan in order to introduce themselves to their fellow citizens, and especially to the Consulate General. It was not worthy at all. They had blamed themselves for having made their address and the neighbor's phone number available to them. For that reason, the girls decided to compensate the neighbor for being kind enough to pass them those in coming calls. From that time on, the girls advised the neighbor to refrain passing them any other phone calls, except if the Consul General himself, decide to call them in order to speak with them personally."

Finally, they said to each other, we actually did not go to Congolese Consulate with the intention of requesting any immediate assistance. Our goal had been to meet our countrymen as the landlord had actually advised us. Besides, our visas are still valid and we had been advised by the School's counselor that all our school requirements have been met, and therefore the school is handling our visas' matters. Girls continued to say to each other, it was just strange for the Consul General to delegate one of his counselors to call us, and reprimand us to such an extent for no apparent reason?

Both were puzzled could not come out with any legitimate explanation. They had wished that the landlord had not advised them to report to the Congolese Consulate in order to establish contact with staff there.

Things had turned out bitter indeed. The girls were really depressed; first of all for the fact that their parents had no concept of their whereabouts at that particular time. Secondly, the neighbors would not allow them to use their telephone to call their country even though they had the money, and they had offered to pay the bill whenever it would arrive. The neighbors were afraid that the bill might exceed their ability to pay.

Shortly afterwards, the same diplomat called again saying, "By the way, I forgot to mention another thing, the Consul General had said to stress upon, "Please remember also that whoever who sent you here in this country, he or she should be the one to handle your consulate matters, not him. Right away, Bipake replied to the diplomat, "Sir, please understand our point. We actually did not come to Consulate office with any intention of requesting any sort of assistance from that office. As far as our legal statuses are concerned, they do not require any immediate change. The reason we had come there was to introduce ourselves to the Consulate General, because your office is a representative of our country to the United Nations.

In addition, it was simple to greet our fellow
Congolese citizens who are living in America, and particularly
in New York City. We actually were advised by friends to take
that action. We had been told that it was necessary that we
follow that protocol of introducing ourselves, formally or
informally to your Consulate. They said, this what every
foreign does, when they get in the foreign land.

Besides, our passports indicate that our tourist visas are
still valid. The reason we had not obtained F-1's or students
visas was due to the fact that the school enrollment was
dependent upon the name of the actual school, which
unfortunately had not been made available to us at that time
until we have arrived in this country. In addition, the School
had confirmed that the change of visas is handled directed by
the School. We are quite aware that the Congolese Consulate
has actually nothing to do with the USA visas or the changes of
statuses. In addition, our passports are newly issued, and their
expirations will take place in four years from now, she said.

Miss Bipake asked the counselor over the phone:
"What really seems to be your main issue with us? Why have
you developed such a high degree of hostility against us?"
Well, the gentleman replied, "nevertheless, the Consul General
said: "Do not bother to report to our Mission anyhow!" The

Second Counselor stressed it. And, then, he hung up the phone.
"Bipake turned to Lunungi and said, "This is amazing, they
said to each other!" How and why would people develop
something out of nothing? This make you wonder, the
intellectual level of our representatives abroad. The country has
such educated people who could actually fill in all these high
diplomatic positions abroad, and why can't they hire them?

Regardless to all those harassments and hostility,
Bipake and Lunungi continued to attend school. They were
very pleased with their English professors. The professors
realized that Bipake and Lunungi were experiencing difficulties
trying to pronounce the Letter, "R" in English which sounded
as a French "R" coming from the throat sound, example in the
word, "Tour" or in the word "Role.

" Another difficulty was the pronunciation of the "TH"
words example, "The or That", both young ladies would
pronounce as, "Zeu meaning the, and "Zat" meaning that". In
helping them to learn the correct pronunciation of the letter R
in the English language, one of their professors began to tease
them, "Remember ladies, you are now in America, not in a
French speaking country; and therefore, we leave our throats
alone. And we pronounce our letter "R" softly not roughly.
We, English speaking people do realize that the French

speaking individuals have a big challenge with the group of word, "The, or That" sound. You have tendency of dropping the letters "Th" and you tend to replace those two letters by a letter "Z" and then, you add a little "e" and little "u" at the end. You probably think that you can fool American English, Oh, no, French speaking people! You just can't do that," laughter! Eventually

practice makes perfect, the young ladies had learnt how to better pronounce the English "R" and the words "The" or "That".

Girls Addressed Concerns to their Parents

Due to the fact that the young ladies could not establish any phone contact with their respective parents, they felt therefore obligated to reach them by correspondence. When they wrote, they actually related all their challenges, chronologically. They began with the negative experience from Mr. Zariap and Mr. Rolog. Secondly, they complained about the awful experience they had just had with the Congolese Consulate in New York City. They reported all the negative statements which came from the Congolese Consulate officials. They also stressed on the fact that the Consul General had forbidden them to ever set their feet in that office again in the future, and that without giving them any legitimate reason.

As soon as their parents received their daughters' correspondence, they became emotionally disturbed. Dismayingly, they made arrangements to transfer money via "European American Banking" at Wall Street's Branch immediately. As usual, the landlady's nephew accompanied them to Wall Street in order to collect their money.

Parents Address Daughter's Complaints to theirForeign Minister

Their parents were very disturbed and brought the complaints to the Foreign Minister, as soon as they had received that complaint. Shortly after that time, a Telex was sent without delay to the Consul General from the office of the Foreign Affairs. The purpose of sending that telex was to verify the authenticity of the complaint received. The Consul General was also asked to report whether or not the young ladies had actually violated any government law since they have arrived in New York City. If this was not the case, then he was asked to explain thoroughly why Congolese citizen should be forbidden to set their feet in a place that is officially known as an extension of the Congo in the foreign land. The last sentence of the telex read, "Your reply is expected within forty eight hours."

The copy of the telex was given to the girls' parents who were already fuming with anger for that sort of abuse to their daughters who were known as decent Congolese citizen.

The same evening that the Consul General received the Telex, he personally decided to call the girls around 9:00 p.m. Unexpectedly, the Haitian roommate came out of her room, and then, called one of the young ladies saying, "Your Consul General is on the phone requesting to speak to you, girls. Bipake and Lunungi said to themselves let us answer the phone, and hear what he had to tell us."

Bipake picked up the phone and said, Hello! And then she heard a male's voice saying diplomatically, "good evening! Is that Bipake or Lunungi?" Bipake answered this is Bipake. Then the voice spoke gently, "I actually must apologize. I am the Consul General, and I am awfully sorry for having missed you; because when you actually came to the Consulate, I was absent, I was in the meeting at the UN. I am sorry that I had missed you, however, I would like you to come tomorrow at the Consulate, precisely, at 12:00 p.m., I would like to meet you, and invite you to have lunch with me. Further, if you have any concerns about your legal documents, he continued please bring them all with you. We will do everything we can to assist you immediately," he said.

The ladies could not understand, why such a sudden change of tone of voice, after having raised hail at them for no apparent reason, causing them miseries for nearly two months.

They were actually frightened to accept his invitation. They decided to decline it, however, after talking it over with their roommate, she had advised them to go anyway and see what the Consul General intend to tell you personally. Bipake and Lunungi were hesitant to go; ultimately, they decided to bring with them their Congolese passports and their high transcripts which their School needed to have it translated officially in English, by their own Consulate.

Since the girls were not really anxious to meet him. Spitefully, they arrived late, and missed the Consul General that day. He had another meeting to attend at the U.N., the girls were advised. Nevertheless, the young ladies experienced totally a different kind of ambiance in that office which was harmonious. The Deputy Consul acted also differently, nicer than he had previously appeared. As soon as he perceived the girls, he saluted them happily, and said to them: "Well, his Excellency, Mr. Uswalu, waited to have lunch with you at 12 p.m, since you could not make it at 12:00 pm., he unfortunately, left for another meetin. However, he had said that, "if you have any documents that need translation you can leave them with us. He will verify the authenticity first, and then, he will decide to proceed.

It was such a relief to the young ladies. They were actually happy that they missed that lunch appointment with the Consul Uswalu. In addition, they felt unsafe to their High School documents and passports at the Consulate. Since they had been skeptical with that environment, they had preferred to bring back their school papers with them until further notice. Shortly after speaking with the deputy consul, they bade him goodbye. However, the girls had a feeling that their complaints had been received by their parents as well as the government officials in the Congo.

Though they had not received acknowledgment of their correspondence from their parents at that time, they were certain however that the reason why the staff treated them courteously lately must have been because of the complaints that had been addressed to their parents and eventually shortly after that period of time, they received a correspondence from their parents. They were informed in details how those issues had been handled legally in the country, right after the complaints were received. It was addressed to the Foreign Minister. They were told the Consul General had to apologize to his Boss for having demonstrated such an immature behavior, for an individual who holds such a position of trust. He admitted that he personally had not seen any offense from the girls, nor had they violated any government's laws since they have been arrived in this country. Their passports were pretty new and their visas were still valid.

He had reported to his Boss to Congo that it was actually the Deputy Consul, who had pushed him to act in a negative way towards the girls, by writing a negative report against the young ladies. Apparently the counselors were somewhat jealous to notice two young ladies who had recently graduated from High School, to actually travel alone to such a huge Country without being accompanied by any adult. In addition, they were also impressed in noticing that they were able to rent a one bed room apartment in a well known borough, called Brooklyn. He also mentioned that the Deputy Consul had wanted him to seize the US Immigration Officials in order to have the girls deported, but I had used my judgment, the Ambassador wrote to his boss, because I saw no legitimate reason to justify such an awful action.

Based on the Consulate General's report, the deputy consul was confronted, and was called back to Congo for having exhibited such a high degree of weakness in handling diplomatic matters in the foreign land.

It was also, for endangering the welfare of their fellow citizens abroad. And he was replaced by a competent individual Mr. Musolo Mingi who held a Master's degree in Political Science, and was able to apply his school knowledge diligently.

Counselor Mutoto's Apology

Finally Mr. Mutoto became self-conscious, and then called the young ladies to apologize for having been an emissary of negative situations. In order to compensate his wrong image, he began asking the girls "Do you by chance know a couple, who worked as missionaries in the Congo for several years, called Mr. and Mrs. Brown?" The girls replied that they actually met them twice. Bipake explained that the first time they met them was for duration of two hours at Kennedy airport.

They also related the circumstance under which they encountered them. Further, she told the gentleman that the second time they saw that couple was on a Wednesday afternoon around 3:00 p.m. in Brooklyn. They actually drove from Connecticut to Brooklyn in order to see the place where they were actually living in.

The missionaries had claimed that the reason they came by, had been to familiarize themselves with the neighborhood, so that the day they would actually decide to invite us, it would be easy for them to drive by and pick us up. Mr. Mutoto screamed and said to the ladies "That was actually the day which the couple came to the Consulate in order to complain against your appearance her in NYC.

Apparently, they have been disturbed to notice two young Congolese girls alone in the USA. They have been inquiring all the necessary details regarding your trip to the United States. Mr. Mutoto continued "I wonder why they didn't ask you all those questions when all of you had already established a clear communication? Probably they were not satisfied with the answers they received from you, and they needed additional elements. That could have been the main reason why they decided to get the Consulate General involved in their search.

Apparently, those so called missionaries, if you examine this matter carefully, it shows that they really had a negative motive in back of their mind, because they acted as though they were instigators. I personally realized that we too, at the Permanent Mission, have been somewhat naïve.

If we had been smart enough, we could have questioned them, and probably, we could have been able to ensnare their hidden intentions." He said: "I think I should really apologize for taking part in that scheme. "I was brought up in a Christian family, I should have known better, not to participate in anysituation which will harm another part of life. And yet, sometimes, you get so caught up in wrong activities and you tend to forget your spiritual obligation. Since all this time, my consciousness has actually been tormenting me. They said that forgiveness is a huge word which frees any individual who would humble himself or herself. Please, girls accept my apology for our Lord's sake. He sounded humble and sincere in his voice.

The young ladies forgave the gentleman for having previously played such an evil role against them. They actually were so grateful to him for having revealed the truth about those missionaries, people who actually detain a spiritual title of honor, the servants of God. Missionaries are expected to follow after our Lord Jesus' footsteps, which is creating harmonious relationship among every human being, and avoiding criticism as well as judgment against each other. It is appalling indeed to notice how some missionaries choose deliberately to misrepresent the truth which the Lord had actually revealed to us.

The young ladies were certainly discouraged, because they had always thought of missionaries to be trustworthy individuals. Nevertheless, they were disappointed about missionaries' misconduct. Who wouldn't be? But their parents had always reminded them, "In life, daughters, you should not dwell on any negative situation or image. You must learn to forgive and forget, because everyone is in reality bound to make a mistake while we still living on this earth. Therefore, it is important to learn to move on, and do not attempt to retrieve your past mistakes or continue to be condemnatory if you wish to succeed in life.

For illustration purpose, Mr. Bipake had occasionally told his narrative regarding the reason why he had become a successful businessman in life. The earliest experience of his employment was appalling indeed. He was exposed to an injustice situation. Although he had been the most qualified individual in that office, and in addition, he was a senior supervisor. And yet, the boss had used him extensively in order to train from scratch, new employees. Those new employees would come in, apparently with a minimum level of education, of less than junior high school. They would exhibit weakness in every sentence they would write in French, although French happen to be their country national language.

In addition, they would come in with no slightest office experience whatsoever. And Mr. Bipake would combine his patience and time to train them step by step. After awhile, those individuals would be promoted, and would gain exorbitant salaries. Further, they would become his superiors, and eventually they would start bossing him around, and also addressing him with an inappropriate language. Viewing such situations, made him very depressed, and as a result, he would go home and begin weeping while talking to his wife just in order to alleviate his pain.

What was the underneath motive? It was simply because, Mr. Bipake was Congolese, and the boss and all those new employees were Belgians. Obviously, it had been very painful, for Mr. Bipake to endure such an injustice for so many years. However, shortly after that, a friend began to invite him to his church. One Sunday, the Sermon of that day was based on "Forgiveness." The Pastor read, **"*Colossians 3:13 Bear with each other and forgive whatever grievances you may have against one another. Forgive as the Lord forgave you*.** Mr. Bipake reported that, after listening to that message, it had stirred his own consciousness. And from that time, he began to pray with the Pastor.

He learned to forgive his boss and everyone else he had trained in that office. And then, he asked God to give him another occupation, which he could perform peacefully. Sure enough, he was inspired to begin some trading. He was able to gather enough money which allowed him to get into a lucrative business. That is how he actually became financially independent. He opened furniture stores in every major city, and hired all types of people including Belgians to work for him. The old company where the boss treated him mean went out of business. Mr. Bipake and Mr. Lunungi became partners, and their precious stones business became very successful. They began travelling nationwide, and back and forth to Brussels, Belgium in order to attend business meetings with his Belgians partners.

CHAPTER IV

Meeting Mr. Paul Magoke and Mr. Franco Filipu

One month later, after the above confusions had ended, another incident happened on a Saturday evening, around 7:30 p.m. The landlord was actually about to come in the young ladies' apartment in order to collect his rent money as usual.

In addition, he had formed the habit of visiting his relatives who lived in the same building.

As soon as he arrived in front of the building that day, he noticed two gentlemen coming out of a Mercedes Benz with a diplomatic plate on it. He noticed that they were attempting to verify the building street address. He stopped suddenly, and observed them for a while; and then, he asked them, "Can I help you with anything? " The strangers replied, "We are here to visit our countrymen from Congo. We believe that this is the right address, but we are not certain."

As soon as the landlord had heard that statement, he replied eagerly, "Oh, I am actually going inside their apartment to visit them as well; let us all go together, he said to both gentlemen." So, they went in together, the landlord introduced them saying "Here are your countrymen. I just met them outside and I brought them over here. He continued good thing I found them, they appeared kind of lost." Bipake and Lunungi were somewhat reluctant to meet them, due to the previous negative experience they had just had with the consulate workers.

Nevertheless, they introduced themselves eagerly. One Gentleman said, "My name is Magoke, Paul I live in Tea Neck, New Jersey.

I am a businessman, and I also work at NASSA. He said it, giggling. The girls got excited over the word, NASSA, and then questioned him, right away, "are you really an astronaut" He replied, "Well, actually I just worked in their administration. I mean at the place where they really launch forth the sky-rockets. Then, shortly after that, the other fellow introduced himself as Mr. Filipu, Franco. He stated that, "I live in Manhattan. I am a First counselor at the Permanent Mission of Congo to the UN." As soon as they heard Franco's introduction, the ladies glanced at each other, and became so alert; and very reserved.

The landlord collected his money, and exchanged conversation for a while with both fellows. Shortly after that, he excused himself and bade them goodbye. So those two Congolese fellows remained there and continued to converse with the young ladies.

Apparently, the counselor noticed that the ladies were not so eager to speak with him. He said, "I was on vacation to Canada visiting my children who study there. Upon my return from my visit to Canada, my wife made me aware of your presence in this city. I understand that you just came from home, he added. I was also told that you had the opportunity to visit our Consulate office.

He continued I am really sorry that I missed you. Mr. Magoke said, "It is actually Franco, who had informed me regarding your arrival here in New York City. Evidently, when I heard Franco mentioned the name "Bipake", I remembered that name from back home. It actually rang the bell in my head. I recall one of my relatives had done

some business with Mr. Bipake's older brother. So, I told Mr. Franco that we should visit them. Bipake is a family friend. This is the reason why we are here to see in which manner we can assist you in this huge city. Mr. Magoke continued we all have had some experience of being a newcomer in a foreign land, or in a city, where you do not really have a close friend or relative to guide you. That could actually be pretty hard at first. That new experience appears as though you have lost your sense of orientation." Mr. Magoke sounded very sympathetic to his newcomers, no wonder he was able to gain their trust.

During their conversation, Mr. Magoke had mentioned the name of Mr.Yungu Magoke, a relative of his, who had done business with Bipake's paternal uncle. Miss Bipake recognized that statement, and confirmed it instantly with her girl-friend Lunungi. Thus, from that moment on, Bipake and Lunungi became relaxed to speak with those gentlemen.

Mr. Magoke said that when he was a lad, he had spent some time at Mr. Ingo's home. That was when he met Bipake's uncle who was dealing with his relative. Magoke also stressed on Bipake's paternal uncle's honesty in doing business with his relative. Well, at that time, Bipake and Lunungi began to feel that they could actually trust Mr. Magoke, as a brother. In fact, that day was the first time that the young ladies had opened up to converse with their countrymen, after having gone through those previous negative experiences with the diplomats and with the so called deceiving missionaries. The conversation was held in such a very good and respectable atmosphere. Bipake and Lunungi were interested in knowing more about Astronauts' experience.

How does it feel like working around those scientists? They started bombarding Mr. Magoke with questions. Mr. Magoke took advantage of newcomers' status, told them nothing but lies. Deep down he eventually regretting for having mentioned this topic, which he knew so little or nothing at all.

Apparently Magoke had no concept regarding the young ladies aptitude. He had no knowledge about the good education which Lyceum, Institut Polytechnique Congolaise offered. Because he had left the city for so long, and the school was created after his departure.

Obviously, he realized from the types of their questions that
those girls were really bright. Magoke felt the heat, and
became somewhat uneasy to continue with the topic which he
had no relevant answers. Consequently, he diverged. Mr.
Franco Filipu just sat there with no comments. He knew
Magoke being confronted, although the girls were honest. They
just wanted to educate themselves in that particular area. When
Magoke and Filipu were about to bid them goodbye, Bipake
and Lunungi asked Mr. Magoke whether or not it was possible
for him to help them find a jewelry maker where they could
sell their semi precious stones in the City?

Hearing the word "precious stones," Mr. Magoke and
Filipu got suddenly excited, and right away, they asked the
girls to exhibit the stones so that they could take a close look of
them. Bipake and Lunungi were so naïve, and innocently, each
of them rushed to her luggage and brought them in the plain
view, before Mr. Filipu and Magoke. Both of them assessed the
stones in their own way. Finally, they concluded that the
stones were genuine. All of a sudden, Magoke exclaimed,
"Oh, I know where I can actually sell them for you! You do
not need to worry.

You can give them all to me. I will go and meet a
friend of mine who is an expert in jewelry industry.

His associates will be glad to buy them all at once. They can buy them at a very good price as well, I assure you," he said. I trust that in less than two days, I will come back to bring you money. He promised them. Bipake and Lunungi were so excited. Their worry about finding a place to sell their stones was over. They felt deep down that Magoke who was their relative's acquaintance was a trustworthy fellow. They had confident that Mr. Magoke could never deceive them. He sounded so sincere according to them. Therefore, they trusted him with all their hearts. Magoke and Fillipu, in fact both appeared so trustworthy gentlemen. After giving the girls an assurance about the business deal, they bade them goodbye. Finally, they promised to see them in two days with the money. The phone numbers and addresses were eventually exchanged easily.

After two days, Magoke who had promised to come back and bring the money, never called the ladies and never showed up. Both girls kept on expecting to hear from him shortly after that, unfortunately, none of them had called the girls. Ultimately, they young ladies took the initiative to call the number Magoke had given them. It turned out that it was a wrong number.

The operator confirmed that the number had been disconnected. The girls had tried to call the Consulate office and asked to speak with Mr. Franco Filipu. Unfortunately, they were told that Mr. Franco Filipu had returned back to Congo, since two days ago now, because his contract had expired.

The ladies kept on hoping to hear from Mr. Magoke somehow in the near future. Unfortunately, days and months and years went by, Magoke just disappeared. .The young ladies decided to leave everything in the hand of God. They knew that one day, somehow, God will bring him back to make that restitution. In the correspondence which the young ladies had received from their respective parents, each letter had a biblical reference. Each parent reminded his daughter, "Do not forget to put God first in whatever you attempt to do there".

You had learned how to say your prayers while you were in our country. Remember to continue doing so. If you have stopped praying, please resume your spiritual activities. You should join a church and be in the community of the believers, so that you do not get involved with the wrong individuals. And remember also that, God wants us to forgive and forget whatever situation that has not brought you happiness. Learn to let go, and move on, this advice helped girls to endure their challenges.

The young ladies blamed themselves for having neglecting their spiritual life. They had recognized their weaknesses, and admitted that the reason they have become so naïve was due to the fact that they did not take the time to seek God in their daily life, thus the confusions took over.

CHAPTER - VI

Young Ladies Moved to their Former Landlord's Sister's Apartment

Bipake and Lunungi blamed particularly their landlord (Mr. Omar) who was always establishing a connection with the wrong people. The landlord had a young sister, who was a Registered Nurse and married to an aggressive man.

She and her husband were renting a four bed room apartment, which was located few blocks away from the building where Bipake and Lunungi had been. Suddenly, it was reported that his sister and her husband had gotten into a very serious domestic violence.

The husband was a man with an intense anger. During the fight, he had broken most of the items in the house, including the TV monitor, chairs and a dinner.

Subsequently the wife seized the police. Therefore, the husband was arrested and was denied legal access to the apartment. Due to the fact that the rent was too high for her alone to maintain the four bedroom apartment, she decided to steal her brother's new tenants, the two African young ladies to come and rent one of rooms. She knew that the young ladies were financially sound, because her nephew had formed the habit of escorting them to collect their money to Wall Street where their money was being wired. She made sure to offer them the biggest room, with two double beds.

Again, the young ladies were naïve. As soon as they visited the room, and the apartment, they immediately liked the place. And they decided to move in within a week. Mrs. Moline appeared to be such an open minded lady. She was extremely happy to have her new African tenants. They had a lot to learn from each other. They talked about history and their cultural connection in order to solidify their relationship.

However, as soon as their previous landlord (Mr. Omar) found out that his own sister had stolen his good tenants, immediately after few days, they got into a serious argument, and they resented each other from that time on. Mrs Moline had four children who had recently come from Haiti.

She also thought it was economical to rent the fourth room to two of her countrymen. However, she was delighted to have those young ladies as her best tenants, because they were able to pay the highest portion of her rent in a timely manner. She also knew that the ladies were receiving money from their parents on a regular basis. The young ladies trusted the landlady very much, because she had assured them, from day one that her home was much safer than their previous place. And therefore, they could feel relaxed, even though the bed room had no lock. Further, she assured them that none of their belongings could ever be in jeopardy. So the young ladies continued to go to school as usual, and leaving everything in plain view in that room. Their money was kept in the handbag; again the girls were naïve due to the fact were leaving the bag with the money in plain view or on the table located in the middle of both beds.

Apparently, they have been under the impression that everything would continue to on smoothly as it had been during the first two months. Obviously, they were shocked to perceive serious problems which had occurred afterwards.

Missionaries' Unexpected Visit and Landlady's Reaction

Few days after their visit to the Consulate, Mr. Brown and his wife were just up to something. They drove from Connecticut to Brooklyn, in the search of the place where they girls were actually staying. Apparently, they had been spiteful, and were curious to find out the manner in which the young ladies had been conducting themselves in that apartment; and whom were they living with. On that particular day however, Bipake and Lunungi, while they were returning home from school, they perceived from the store window, beautiful winter dresses which were displayed parallel to each other. The girls were attracted to that display's view, and then, entered the store in order to buy those dresses.

That small store, unfortunately, did not provide any fitting room. And therefore, both girls took the chance to purchase the dresses randomly, without knowing whether or not the sizes would be appropriate. So, as soon as they arrived in their room, anxiously they began trying them on. Unexpectedly, the missionaries arrived in front of the apartment. At that time, each of them had on her newly purchased dress with all the tags attached.

However, few minutes later, the landlady's daughter, suddenly, knocked at their bedroom door. Bipake then rushed to open the door, and then, heard the little girl saying, "Come out quickly, my mother said that you have guests outside who wish to see you, immediately." The young ladies were taken by surprise, for they knew nobody in their new community, who could be asking to see them immediately, around 3:00 p.m., and besides, it was in the middle of the week.

Nevertheless, they had no choice but to rush out, and see who those people actually were. At their amazement, they had noticed Mr. and Mrs. Brown standing next to their car, and ready to just walk inside the apartment. So, the young ladies were compelled to go out, all dressed up in their new outfits, with the tags hanging out. Surprisingly, they saw them, and greeted them. Amazingly, they were not apologetic for that disruption. Own their own volition, they offered the reason of their visit, saying: "Oh we just wanted to see where you are staying, so that the day we will come to pick you up, we will know exactly where to find you."

Almost, all the neighbors were attracted to witness that peculiar view. Shortly afterwards, they realized that they were not welcome inside the apartment, so they bade them goodbye, and drove away.

After that, the young ladies returned to their room. They said to each other, this is strange, indeed. They wondered why the missionaries would want to drive all the way from Connecticut to Brooklyn all of a sudden to merely come and see where we are actually staying and whom we are living with?"At that time, Bipake and Lunungi were not aware that, the couple had already gone to the Congolese Consulate in order to raise some issue. However, the landlady and her relatives made some remarks about missionaries' unexpected visit.

The Landlady Reprimanded the Tenants for Missionaries' Unexpected Visit

She told the young ladies that in the future, if they were expecting visitors, they were supposed to notify the landlady, prior to their arrival to her apartment. After reprimanding them, the landlady seized that opportunity to advise Bipake and Lunungi. She told them to be very cautious regarding anyone whom they are actually bringing in her house. She said to them, your guests actually wanted to access my house, as soon as they got out of their car, but I had asked them to wait for you outside.

It is not that I am attempting to act mean, but you are newcomers here. And therefore, I feel that I must sound a warning to you. It is actually because I realize that as newcomers, you have no concept how people behave here. Shortly after that remark, Bipake replied right away, "Mrs. Moline, We must apologize for this inconvenience, indeed. Please believe me that we actually were not expecting this couple, by all means. In fact, we had just met this couple no longer ago. It was precisely, last week when we had gone to the airport in order to meet our friend, who was going to our country on a family emergency.

The couple in question happens to be her family's friends. We were told that they had been missionaries in our country for a long duration. Currently, they are retired, and live in Connecticut. The landlady replied with a sarcastic tone of voice, "I don't care whether they are missionaries of what! What I am telling you, is just to be extra careful while you are here in this city, and especially while you are residing in my house. Further, bear in mind that many people utilize different types of labels in order to introduce themselves, and gain access in your home. And subsequently, individual would shortly cause you unnecessary dilemma. My basic concern is the fact that you are not quite sure of the types of individuals you are dealing with.

Further, you do not know exactly the motive which lies behind that visit, until it is too late to remedy the situation." She spoke with audacity, shaking her head up and down, with her eyes quasi-closed.

Furthermore, she added, "I have children in this house, as you can notice; and believe me, I do not wish to have any problem with my children." In addition, she continued you said that those people told you that they live in Connecticut; but do you know that Connecticut is quite a distance from Brooklyn? How could they just decide to drive in here, under the guise to just come and take familiarize themselves with the neighborhood.

They surely have some peculiar intention, the landlord commented. She was panic stricken apparently. Finally, she continued being a nurse, you see, I have some degree of psychology. And I can sense any hidden motive. And I still feel that this is a weird visit! Regardless to their hidden motive, you girls should really tell them that next time they plan to come by, they are required, out of courtesy, to notify you prior to driving in here. I just did not feel comfortable seeing them abruptly like that," she added, shaking her heard from left to right.

She continued it is not a good idea for visitors to just come in unexpectedly, as though they were driving in their private field, the landlady appeared really annoyed with such view. In addition she said, "Look at your own appearance, it just isn't appropriate for your guests to see you dressed up in these new outfits with tags hanging on each side. You have just come from school apparently; and surely you stopped in a store, and each one purchased a dress. This is absolutely not an acceptable manner of taking people by surprise as though they are up to some fishy mission. Supposed you had been out, your guests would have missed you eventually, do you get my point? The landlady added. In order to clarify this issue, Lunungi replied, "Mrs. Moline as you have just noticed us walking in from school.

We had just bought each a winter dress from that small store in the corner. Since the store has no fitting room, we had just purchased the items without trying them on. Believe us, Mrs. Moline that we really were not expecting that couple's visit, by all means. Besides, they had never indicated that they would drive here without noticing us. Mrs. Moline, our appearance actually confirms our point. We are in the midst of fitting our new dresses on, and no interruption was expected on their part.

We are as just surprised as you and your children are."
Bipake added, "We were actually so embarrassed to walking
outside and to meet that couple with dresses full of tags,
hanging all over. In fact, no one can actually think about fitting
new clothes if that individual knows that the guests will be
arriving at that moment, "laughter! O.K, Mrs. Moline said, I
understand, but just be careful in the future. Ultimately, that
incident was settled right then.

Missionaries' Invitation and Declined of Invitation

Few weeks after Mr. Mutoto, the Congolese diplomat
had taken the initiative to apologize to the girls, as well as
revealing the whole truth regarding the missionaries' mischief
the young ladies received a note by mail from the couple, Mr.
and Mrs. Brown.

The note read: *Dear friends: "We will pick you up one
of these days to spend a weekend with us, as we had actually
promised you." Sign Mr. & Mr. Brown. After having read the
couple's letter, Bipake and Lunungi decided to seize this
opportunity, and to reply, affirming that their invitation has
actually been declined for personal reasons. Bipake wrote:
"Dear Mr. and Mrs. Brown. Thank you for your invitation.*

We were very happy to meet you at the airport. We were glad to hear that you had retained a very good experience with the Congolese friends, and that you still keep in touch with them. We were impressed to notice that you had taken the time to drive from Connecticut to Kennedy airport to meet our friend Maseko. In addition, you sent gifts to your best friends in the Congo. You really have exemplified the love of God. However, we wish to remind you that when we met at the airport, we communicated clearly and harmoniously. As a matter of fact, you had asked us all the questions pertaining to our trip, and ultimately our arrival to the USA. All your questions were answered thoroughly. You also had wanted to find out whether or not my friend and I are being sponsored by any church, any special organization or a government agency. We had also made it clear that we have not been awarded any sort of scholarship that brought us here, but from our own parents' efforts. Mr. Zariap and Rolog from the Wall Street office, could very well certify this fact, if need be. They would tell everyone who is concerned about us, and regarding our trip arrangements to New York City. Further, those individuals would have also to indicate the reason of their concerns.

In fact, we do not quite understand; what seems to disturb you about our coming to this country? What have we done that appears to bother every one of you really?

We have not gone to anyone's home to seek for a shelter or money. Likewise, we have not been to any church to apply for any scholarship or food. So far we have been self-sufficient and living moderately. We are just wondering, Mr. and Mrs. Brown, what are your reasons of going behind our backs, and especially going to the Congolese Consulate in the attempt to find more physical evidence of our being here in this city. Apparently you have been very busy, going around asking everyone how, and why, and who send us here? What is your motive behind all these questioning? Because you do not trust us, we also cannot trust you. And therefore, we regret to inform you that we have declined your invitation. And please, do not reiterate your invitation, because it will not be honored for the above mentioned reasons.

Sincerely,

Bipake and Lunungi.

Mr. and Mrs. Brown's Reaction to the Young Ladies' Letter

As soon as the couple received this letter, they were embarrassed for they realized that their secret was exposed to their prospective guests, prior to their invitation. And therefore, in order to cover up their mischief, they decided to make a copy of that letter, and mailed it to Maseko to Seattle, where she was studying in order to complain about Bipake and Lunungi's reactions to their invitation. After reading the copy of that letter, Maseko promised them to reprimand the young ladies for writing such unkind letter to missionaries. Bipake and Lunungi wrote back to Maseko, and reminded her the following facts, "do not forget, you are here, because the churches' awarded you a scholarship. Those missionaries are all aware of that situation. In our case however, we feel that we do not have to be subject to any suspicious, harassment and hostility from anyone, because we know that we owe nothing to anybody, except to our own parents. We both know exactly that our parents are earning their living honestly. They are endeavoring to support their daughters in the foreign land. Maseko, you know quite well that the couple left our country since 1958. They do not know what type of business our fathers actually do for living.

Apparently, missionaries are not ready to believe that, after 1960, things have been developed differently. And that Lunungi or Bipake's fathers can have enough money to support their children in the foreign land. They really need to go back recently and see the change that had taken place since they last were there. Evidently, Maseko knew what kind of families Bipake and Lunungi came from, but the couple and the counselors had no concept regarding that issue. This letter had actually sealed that entire scenario.

Disappearance of the White Bag and Money

The landlady had formed the habit of collecting her rent money from the young ladies on the last day of the month. On that particular day however, the young ladies had faced a conflict of schedule. Normally, the agent at the bank would notify them whenever their money transfer had been performed for them to come and collect it. Generally, whenever they received the bank notice, the girls would miss class that day, and would go to Wall Street, accompanied by their landlady's nephew, who enjoyed walking with them to that area. When the banker had called them that day to report to the bank in order to receive their money, they had realized that they had a conflict in their schedule.

Taking a final English exam was crucial to them, and on the other hand, paying the rent on that last day of the month, way very important as well, based on the contract they had with the landlady. Due to the fact that the landlady expected to receive her money on that last day of the month, without fail, the girls decided to make her aware of that conflict of schedule.

Apparently she understood, and commented that, "I do not care as long as your money has already arrived at the bank. You can pay me tomorrow as soon as you receive it." The excuse was accepted. On the following day, the money was collected from the bank. As soon as they had arrived in the apartment, Mrs. Moline, the landlady and her children were seating right in the living room. She was very eager to see them coming in, and jokingly, she said, I assumed you have brought all the money from the bank?"

Bipake and Lunungi replied as a matter of fact, we might as well just stop prior to accessing our room, and pay our rent. Again, the girls were so naïve the fact that they had just open the envelope which was received from the bank, with full of new hundred dollars bills in front of everyone seated in the living room. Bipake pulled out the exact amount of money needed to pay the rent while everyone was observing, and gave it to Mrs. Moline.

After having made their payment, they proceeded to their bed room.The landlady was extremely happy, so were her children, who appeared as though they were spectators at the time the money was being given. They all had a big smile; observing their mother receiving money from their new African tenants. All of them appeared cheerful indeed.

The next day, prior to leaving the house for school, the young ladies recalled their landlady's advice concerning the protection of their money, "Not to carry so much money in your purse, while you are going out, because there are so many chiefs out there. They could easily snatch it from your hands, so you need to be careful in this regard."

Apparently, the landlady acted initially as such a very good advisor to those newcomers. She warned them repeatedly, "Remember to carry just a little amount of money needed for that day. Leave most of it at home." She insisted, repeatedly. And therefore, they began to leave a great portion of their money in a medium size white bag. That bag was always placed on the small table, which was stationed in between each bed. The bag has several compartments. The young ladies felt that Mrs. Moline was actually being so protective of them at first.

So, they learnt to carry only enough money to spend for the day, and left a large portion of it in the in that white bag in their room them, because they knew that they could never be replaced for all eternity. The girls were terribly affected, because they knew they will never see some of their classmates' faces again, due to circumstance of life. The memory was gone! The girls could not wait the return of the owner of that house, Mrs. Rose Moline, so that they could inquire the whereabouts of that famous white bag.

They waited impatiently; however, Mrs. Moline and her children were still out until 9:00 p.m. that day, opposed to 4:00 p.m. It was suspicious indeed the bag with the money was completely missing. Bipake said, "This has never occurred since we have moved in this room, besides, Mrs. Moline and her children have never been out this late during the week. What had happened today?" Lunungi agreed with her. Was it a coincidence or it was a conspiracy? It was indeed questionable. Nevertheless, they waited impatiently for Mr. Moline and her children's return.

The landlady and her children had arrived that day around 9:30 p.m. Bipake and Lunungi gave them an hour to rest, prior to approaching the owner.

Basically, around 10:30 p.m., Bipake and Lunungi went to see her in order to inquire about the white bag. Even though, the young ladies had approached Mrs. Moline calmly and politely, her reaction had been, nevertheless, violent! Apparently, her nervous reaction showed that she was guilty. "Sarcastically, she answered, "What do you mean by saying that you do not find your white bag with the money?" Who are you attempting to accuse, me or my children?" The white bag was lying on the small table when we left. Whatever happened to it, she insisted, "My children and I do not know anything about your white bag, o.k.?" Mrs. Moline repeated the same sentence over and over. Her children stood there, observing as spectators would.

Lunungi told Mrs. Moline, "We know the money is already gone, as we speak. But it would be appreciated, if the individual who took the bag could return the pictures which were placed in that big compartment. Those are our s high school classmates' pictures. We beg you, Madam; those pictures are the only thing that we are actually requesting from you." Saying these words, Bipake and Lunungi began to weep, as they had made the attempt to convince Mrs. Moline about those important pictures.

In addition, they said to the owner those pictures are actually from our childhood, they are of the highest value to us; because they can never be replaced, for all eternity. Life is unpredictable, you would never know.

We might not ever get to see those high school friends any longer. At least, we can keep their souvenirs. Further, one of the girls continued Mrs. Moline please, understand that the value of those pictures worth more than anything else to us. Regardless to their plea, Mrs. Moline continued to scream her head off, in order to hide her own guilty consciousness, apparently. There had been no legitimate explanation in regard to the white bag's disappearance.

Evidently, Bipake and Lunungi appeared annoyed and confused, because Mrs. Moline's response seemed irrelevant. Girls were evidently depressed, because they had been exposed to several challenges since day one of their arrival in this city already. In the light of this situation, they became convinced finally that the white bag including its contents were eventually gone forever. They again, took the blame, and realized that they have been very naïve. Why had they possibly trusted the landlady in the first place? Why hadn't they sensed that she was attempting to approach them cunningly, certainly, underneath, she had bad intentions.

It was obvious, because the landlady kept on insisting that they should make sure to leave a big amount of money in the house, and carry just a little bit in the purse. Why didn't we suspect that this woman had a wrong motive in the first place, especially the fact that she had left this bed room without any lock?

The girls concluded that probably the reason people have been taking advantage of them all that time was due to the fact that they had neglected turning to God in order to seek his guidance and protection. Apparently, Bipake said to Lunungi, all these experiences seem like the awakening time. Lunungi added, I recalled, the sermon which Pastor Zaché had preached on the last Sunday we attended church. He said, "God does permit certain situations in life, if he notices that that individual's faith in him tends to weaken." God has to give that individual a spiritual push, so to speak, so that he or she could be awaken and seek God's will. Bipake said to her friend, "that Sunday was not the first time for me to hear the awakening time's Sermon. My mother said that Pastor Zaché loves to preach that Sermon. That is the reason why you had noticed the congregations of Congolese Mothers had been growing stronger and stronger in terms of their faith. That is what is being called *THE AWAKENING TIME*.

My mother made sure to advise me, on that last evening prior to our departure, she said, " my daughter, remember as you are going away, everything in this world comes and goes, but the word of God is the only thing that will remain in somebody's life for eternity. Therefore in whatever you do in life, ***DO NOT FORGET TO PUT GOD FIRST***. Lunungi commented my mother as you know has really been growing spiritually since she joined the congregation of Congolese Mothers. She too reminded me to do the same. However, it is now up to us to put things we have been reminded into practice. Both of us need to be awakened currently. We should begin placing God first prior to doing anything, surely this would prevent us attracting all these wrong individuals. As the old saying, "Female individuals have strong intuitions, your mother and my mother both knew we would really need this simple but important advice, Lunungu told her friend.

Chapter - VI

The Instructor Introduces the Young ladies to Mrs. Elombe

A week after the vanishing of the white bag at the landlady' house, the young ladies continued with their school activities. When they arrived at school one day, the divine providence opened another door for the girls. It was almost at the end of the class's activities, when one of the instructors came across another female African Student. She was known as Mrs. Elombe from Liberia. The lady was married to a Congolese man. The instructor seized the opportunity to introduce the young ladies to Mrs. Elombe. He said: "Ladies, I would like you to meet Mrs. Elombe. Her husband is one of your countrymen, she had told me." The lady confirmed indeed that she was from Liberia, but her father was German and her mother was from Liberia. She also confirmed that her husband came from the Democratic Republic of Congo. She spoke highly about her husband, giggling every time she talked about him. Further, she said that her husband had been a diplomat in her country, five years ago. Furthermore, she stated that they met during the time he had worked there. Moreover, she added that her husband and her had been married for five years, and had one beautiful and bright son.

Mrs. Elombe asked the girls, "Where do you live? The young ladies replied that they were renting a room in Brooklyn, on Eastern Parkway area. The lady said to them that her place was on Empire Boulevard, and that it was not far from they were. Mrs. Elombe was curious, and she wanted to know whether or not they were happy at the place where they were renting.

Actually, it had been two days ago since that awful incident occurred. Apparently, they felt helpless and heartbroken. Since the girls were deeply depressed, they seized the opportunity to relate their negative experience to Mr. Elombe.

Upon hearing that incident, she was very touched. She knew that the landlady took advantage of them. When she arrived at her home that evening, she immediately related the incident to her husband. He knew that the young ladies were newcomers, and that the landlady had been taking advantage of them. Her husband also was deeply concerned. He knew how it is like being a newcomer in the foreign land. One would actually need all the necessary assistance in order to get settled. Mrs. Elombe was such a bright and kind woman, she pushed her husband to get a hold of one of his friends and help the girls to get out of that woman's place immediately.

Mr. Elombe, got on the phone, and called one of his countrymen, who had been his long time buddy. He made him aware of the situation. His buddy and Mr. Elombe got together, and decided to find a solution to move the ladies from Mrs. Moline's home immediately, and before she causes them further abuses. His buddy and himself, called the girls the next day. They decided to pick them up around 7:30 p.m. and drove them to the home of another countryman in order to inquire about any vacancy in his three-story house. His house was also located in Brooklyn, but far away. The man was half Angolan and half Congolese. He was a US citizen. However, some of his relatives were still living in the Congo. His wife was an American citizen and they had a seventeen year old son

The man was very eager to see his fellow citizens in this country. He had a one bed room vacant apartment which they began to rent at a reasonable price. His wife was so curious to meet ladies from her husband's country. He reported, jokingly to the girls that his friends as well as his own wife had always teased him, "We have never met women from your country, Mr. Buti. How do they look like? They probably are ugly.

Perhaps you are just ashamed to introduce them to us." Mr. Buti was so proud of his countrymen, because the young ladies had beautiful figures, as well as their appearance. Besides, they were well educated. His wife could not help confessing that she had never met youth or female from her husband's country. She started to observe them from head to toe, and noticed that they were refined with full of mannerism. In addition, they spoke politely. They were dressed up with taste. Further, Mrs. Buti continued to confess that, "I have been giving my husband a hard time, laughing.

In fact, whenever he did something wrong, I would tell him that, "I really should divorce you, and send you back to Africa where you would have to marry your ugly African woman," Laughter! Mr. Buti replied, "Yes, that is what my wife and my friends always tell me. I actually pitied them, because of lack of opportunity to travel and see the world, and draw a conclusion on their own." I have often urged them to put a couple of dollar each month aside until they have gathered enough money to travel abroad. This would indeed help you people to acquire a new perspective, but they won't listen.

Mr. Elombe and his buddy related the young ladies' negative experience to Mr. Buti, which they had just had from Mrs. Moline's home. They told him how the landlady had just robbed the poor innocent girls. They also told him that the young ladies are very serious, they are here to study, and their parents are well to do in the Congo.

Obviously, the young ladies were so grateful first to their school's instructor for introducing them to Mrs. Elombe; in addition, they were very grateful to Mrs. Elombe and her husband for helping them establish another connection with Mr. Buti. The ladies moved from Mrs. Moline's apartment to their countryman's family home. They had noticed that the apartment was well kept and roomy. In addition, the rent was very reasonable. He was in his early sixty, and had a happy demeanor in general. He was called Mr. Thomas Buti.

Chapter - VII

The Young Ladies Moved to Mr. Thomas Buti's House

Mr. Buti was proud of his countrymen. And therefore, he developed the habit of visiting his new tenants, and began to instruct them how to avoid trouble with people in this country. He always referred to the negative experience, which the girls had had with Mrs. Moline, their second landlord.

Further, he warned the young ladies to be cautious, "Don't you ever accept to co-sign any legal documents or any paper pertaining to receiving credits for so call friends. Because you are newcomers, when you do not know the law of the country, you would definitely make mistakes that cannot be remedied. Mr. Buti, related his own experience and those of his personal friends from Angola as well as those originated from the Democratic Republic of the Congo. He said, "Girls do not be ignorant as I and my friends had been. As newcomers, our American girlfriends took advantage of us. Each of us was asked by his girl-friend to co-sign their legal documents which would allow them in getting credits, from the bank, or any creditors, furniture, jewelry or clothing stores.

Each of us was bombarded with unexpected bills. When we began to argue about paying those high bills, as a result, we were each taken to Court. Consequently, the Court authorized credits companies to begin garnishing each one of us. It actually took years for me as well as my countrymen to actual finish paying our girl-friends' high credit bills. The pressure was too much on us that each of us began actually weeping for not having anyone to warn us regarding the consequence of signing legal papers erroneously.

Apparently, none of us could have any savings for such a long time. The girl-friends began mocking us, "yes newcomers, African men, and let us take advantage of you, while we can! We all had a language problem, and therefore, we were ignorant of the law of the country. Certainly, that the main reason why newcomers in general make unnecessary mistakes, it is because they are ignorant of the law of country. The law applies whether you are ignorant or wise. I am so glad for you, girls, because you are motivated to going to school and study English. However, you should learn how to ask questions prior to doing anything, especially before signing any legal paper or document for whoever it may be. Truly, I am notifying you these things in order to prevent you from making similar mistakes; I and my friends had erroneously made awful mistakes in this country out of ignorance.

In the foreign land, he continued remember always that a newcomer appears as though he or she is stupid, but it is not really stupidity; it is rather a lack of adequate information of that land. And therefore, it is important to be familiar with the law of the country. This would help you to respect it fully, and to prevent any discrepancy while leaving in that country. Mr. Buti was so protective of the girls. He overdid it, and too much of it eventually became a nuisance to the ladies at the end.

The Landlord's Regular Visit and Frustration

Mr. Buti formed the habit of visiting the girls between the hours of 7:30 p.m. and 8:30 p.m. He was accustomed to noticing girls' main activities, which were sometimes, doing their English home works, or sometimes watching television. Basically, whenever he stopped by, he hardly sat down. He would just stand and chat with them for a while, and then, he would return back to his apartment.

However, his wife used to encourage the young ladies to pay them an informal visit from time to time as well. But Girls were so accustomed to being independent that they hardly went to the landlord's apartment unless they were invited informally or formally.

Because he was so protective of the ladies, Mr. Buti had always wanted to see them around their house, every evening he would stop by their place. Gradually, the young ladies began associating with their classmates. Their friends started to invite them for social gathering, such as a birthday's occasion. Mr. Buti who was so accustomed seeing the young ladies staying at home on the weekends, started to act so peculiar, whenever the young ladies would go out at their friends birthdays parties. Mr. Buti had the key to their apartment. He would get in whenever they were absent, between the hours of 7:30 p.m.- 8:30 p.m. He would be so furious at them. Why aren't they here around this hour? He would be disturbed. He would keep on checking every now and then, to see whether or not they have returned.

He would actually continue to check until sometimes after 10:00 p.m. In order to alleviate his anger, if he noticed that they were still out around that time, he would open their closet, and take out everything from the closet, such as clothes, linens, coats, shoes, handbags, books, notebooks, pens, including kitchen utensils sometimes, and he would pile them up in the middle of the living room. They would actually appear as an *Egyptian Pyramid*. The minute you would walk in the apartment, you would notice a tremendous, huge mountain of all those stuffs staring at you! In fact, his justification would be "You girls are probably board to death, and that is probably why you are going out, and staying too late. In order to keep busy, you should find something to do around your own house and keep out of trouble. I do this to help you and not to hurt you." It is appalling that you do not quite understand me.

Apparently such action would make the girls very depressed, because they were just tenants even though they were countrymen. Watching that pyramid of clothing, girls would realize that it would actually require herculean energy to begin selecting each item, and put it in its proper place. And therefore, they would keep quiet without asking the landlord anything. At first they used to put back items right after the landlord had messed it up.

Finally, they decided not to remove the Pyramid right after his action, but to let it stay there for over a month without touching it. They used to pick up from the pile, whatever was needed at that time, and let that herculean mountain stay there for months so that every time he came by, he could enjoy looking at his unfortunate action. Because the young ladies would give him an absolute silence for his childish behavior, the landlord would feel guilty conscious.

His consciousness would start bothering him then he would start shouting before his wife. "Now, I look to them as though I were their enemy. Me, Buti, they are resenting me! I have been nice to them, all this time. I let them rent my apartment at a moderate amount of money. I have never stolen any of their money as did their previous landlady, so called Mrs. Moline, whom they have been complaining about. The girls are not grateful at all, the fact that they are not talking to me any longer, this is a confirmation that they are naughty, he would tell his wife.

The girls would continue to ignore him for quite sometimes. His wife would be laughing at the entire scenario. And would finally advise the young ladies, "Do not mind him just put back your stuff in the closet and the book on the table. Take your time, I understand the pain and the stress my husband is putting you through. It is not fun at all, she would confirm. She would continued it is quite annoying to coming from outside and finding all this huge mountain of clothing and other mixed stuff in the middle of the apartment, staring at you as Monster."Then the girls would seize that opportunity to reply to the landlord's wife, "Mrs. Buti, we could understand if we were not paying any rent here. But the rent is being honored on time. Besides, we are independent tenants. Therefore, we feel that coming from the same country, does not exclude the fact that we are here just because we are paying the rent. We should not feel as though we have to ask his permission in order to go out when our classmates invite us. His concept is just unbecoming indeed."

Mrs. Buti, Lunungi said it, emphatically, "We are not his wives or his girl-friends. It is you who are his wife. We can understand if he would be jealous at you going out without notifying him. His behavior would be justified effectively. And then, Bipake added, yes, Mrs. Buti, please tell your husband to stop acting in this manner. If he does not want us to continue renting his apartment, please tell him to let us know. We would inquire around and God will help us find another place. It is just obnoxious to experience such things around the house. It is unbearable and repugnant, Bipake added, crying. What an awful experience, we have to go through! Lunungi concluded. Gradually, the anger would start fading away and the young ladies would eventually begin putting things at their appropriate place.

CHAPTER VIII

Meeting Ms. Ndaya Kati from Upper Manhattan

One day, Bipake and Lunungi received an unexpected phone call from a Congolese young lady who was studying at Columbia University. She was renting a small studio apartment there. She introduced herself as Kitamasi Kati. She told Bipake and Lunungi how she actually got their phone number from Mr. Buti's acquaintance.

Further, she expressed her joy, saying "I am so overwhelmed to hear that there are two other young ladies from my country, who are studying here, besides from myself. She insisted that she wanted to meet them absolutely, as soon as possible. Bipake and Lunungi were somewhat apprehensive due to all those negative experiences they have been going through. They were not so eager about meeting their countrymen any longer.

However, Kati was not aware of their experience, and she kept on calling them on a regular basis. Finally, two months later, they had arranged to get together. She first invited them at her place at Columbia University. Eventually, they all had a good time, and then, she offered a gift to each one of them, prior to bidding them goodbye.

Bipake and Lunungi confessed that they overreacted when Ndaya had first called them. However, they had realized that after all, it had turned out to be a very positive association. And therefore, they kept in close contact from that moment on. They began calling each other regularly, at least once every two weeks. Six months later, Ndaya had called her friends saying that, I would like to visit you at your place. Her friends replied "We too, were actually planning to invite you over, but for the time being, we are preparing SAT Exams, and certainly, we would get together as soon as the exams are over."

Apparently, she understood at that time, however, a week later, she had called them again, saying, "I really want to see you my friends. I will be at your place tomorrow, Thursday. You do not have to worry about giving me any travelling directions to your place, because I am quite familiar with that area, and I know which train goes there," she said. Her friends provided her with their schedule of that week. Further, the girls advised her the time which they were scheduled to arrive home on that day.

Both friends were prepared to welcome her. And therefore, around 4:30 p.m., she had arrived with a small luggage. Neither Bipake nor Lunungi expected Ndaya to stay overnight with them, because in all her conversations, she had never alluded that she was going to stay overnight. So Bipake and Lunungi rushed to prepared dinner, because they had both been under the impression that their guest would actually return back to her place, after the meal had been served.

After dinner, however, they started watching television, and carrying on making various comments. Ndaya actually appeared to be very relaxed, and showed no urgent intention to return home. She had taken her high heels off, and slippers were provided her. Bipake and Lunungi noticed that it was getting very late, and yet, she was not alluding to return home nor did she indicate her intention to move in with them. So, Bipake asked her would you like us to accompany you at Subway station. Ndaya replied, "Oh, well, I can stay with you overnight, if you do not mind." Hearing this request, Bipake and Lunungi accepted it. However, they thought that it was going to be just for that one night. And therefore, they provided her with all the necessary things needed, such as a night gown, towels and a tooth brush. The couch was fixed for her to sleep in the living room. She felt very comfortable with the girls.

The next day however, Bipake had class on that Friday, whereas Lunungi did not. So on that Friday, Bipake left for school, bidding Ndaya goodbye, because she thought that Kati was going to return home, while Bipake was still at school. Lunungi stayed behind with Kati, she prepared breakfast for the guest. She had thought that Ndaya will express the intention of leaving right after breakfast, but it was not the case. Kati just sat there, watching television and carrying on diverse conversations with Lunungi.

Suddenly, Lunungi realized that it was getting to lunch time. So she decided to prepared lunch for all of them. After, lunch time Lunungi was expecting Kati to bid her goodbye, nevertheless, Ndaya wouldn't utter such word. Around 5:00 p.m., Bipake arrived from school. It truly was shocking to notice that Kati Ndaya was still there. As soon as Ndaya saw Bipake coming in, she greeted her happily, and asked inquired regarding her day's school activities, "how was school today?" Bipake sat down with her and started carrying on conversation while Lunungi was preparing dinner.

In reality, Kati was some sort of a chatter box. She actually spoke nonstop, and never had time to listen, but to carry the lead. So after the dinner time went by, still Ndaya did not initiate her desire to return home. Therefore, she stayed again overnight. She really felt at home, and knew how to fix her own bed in the living room.

In evening of Saturday, Ndaya's routine went on. They had breakfast, and then later on lunch was served. Right after lunch, Kati told both young ladies: "I will be stepping out for a while, but I shall return later. Hearing this statement, Bipake seized the opportunity to question her, "Ndaya you have just said that you will come back today, later?" Instead of answering either with a simple "yes" or "no", Ndaya raised an amazing scene; because that question sounded as a confrontation to her.

She suddenly placed her bag on the chair located by the doorway. She then turned to Bipake, angrily. She stared at her for few minutes, and then, she replied, "What do you really mean Bipake? Why are you questioning me whether or not I will be returning again later? At that time, both of her hands were placed on her waist; while she was verifying Bipake's question. She was shaking her head up and down. She was sweating and fuming.

That is very disrespectful, she went on. You do not actually treat a friend in such indecent manner. When you came at my place, I received you appropriately. You departed from my house happily. Why then, make a friend feel unwelcomed at your place? Kati twisted things around in order to carry on the argument.

She continued evidently, Lunungi had better mannerism than you Bipake. She added, audaciously, "Yes" I will be returning here tonight, if this is what you wish to know! Don't you see my luggage laying here? Do you see me going out with it? Of course, I will come back, because you are aware that I am staying here, and you should not have asked that unsuitable question," Ndaya replied.

Lunungi and Bipake looked at each other quietly, and they could not believe their eyes and their ears. Here we go again, as they watched Ndaya leave with her hand bag, and leaving her small luggage behind. That was an indication that certainly she will return, and she will be staying again overnight. On Sunday, Kati was still there with the girls. It was peculiar to the girls to notice that Kati has spread their telephone number to practically everyone of her friends and acquaintances, during that short duration.

Unfortunately, she did that without requesting their permission. She was receiving phone calls from practically everyone she knew. *She was receiving more calls than Bipake and Lunungi who were the owners of the apartment. It was strange to the, because their* home sounded as though it had become a business office. Another weird thing was that every time the phone rang, she would rush to answer the call.

She would say to the girls, "Let me answer that call, if they ask one of you girl, I will pass the call to whomever it belong to. Bipake and Lunungi were puzzled and helpless with this new scenario. They could not understand such a peculiar behavior.

Few days later, the landlord, Mr. Buti and his wife had noticed that Kati was still in the girls' apartment. That brought his attention, and he went by to verify the fact. "What is happening here?" The landlord asked seriously. "Has Kati moved with you girls or what?" Bipake and Lunungi said, well we do not quite understand this scenario either. She had called us on last Thursday, stating that "I will be there to visit you." We actually had wanted her to visit us within two weeks when we will be finished with our college entrance exam, but we could not understand why she insisted to come here on last Thursday.

As you noticed, Bipake said, she has been with us since last Thursday until today, Sunday. She just went out for a while, and she had promised to return again later. Bipake continued, yesterday she had started an argument with me just, because prior to going out, I had heard her indicating the desire to return again later today, later. When I had verified her statement to return again, she actually grew very upset with me. So I asked her, "Are you planning to return again here tonight? "She was actually offended, because I had put the question in that manner. She answered to me sarcastically, "You know very well that I am staying here with you, how are you questioning, whether or not I shall return again today?"

Hearing this statement, the landlord spoke firmly, saying, "This apartment is only for two people, you and Lunungi. I will not rent this one apartment to three women. You women are trouble makers. We men cannot trust you. Three women in one apartment will entail that I will be calling the Police Department practically every second to settle your disputes, because women fight like cats and dogs. I do not want her to live here with you, by all means. I cannot afford to keep three Cats in one place, because they will eventually scratch each other.

You tell Ndaya, as soon as she gets back to come, and see me. I have one room available in my apartment. If she needs a place to rent, she can rent it. I will not charge her a high rent. My rent is always reasonable to all of my tenants. I am a Christian, I pray to God. I want to go to Heaven when I die; that is why I always keep in good terms with my fellow beings. Though, some people think that I am a nasty person, because some time I lose my temper. But I do not just get angry without any legitimate reason.

I know, I have a very good heart," he added. It was true that the landlord was a good hearted person, besides from his crazy actions sometimes. He was a religious person, every Sunday he and his wife would be all dressed up to go to church and worship God. He was not a resentful individual either.

Young Brother (Simon Buti) Visits Landlord

The Landlord's invited his brother who had moved from Angola to Congo, during the civil war. His brother had actually postponed several invitations from Mr. Buti. It had been more than five times he postponed his arrival to New York. The landlord was overwhelmed the day his brother accepted his invitation, and confirmed his arrival. He announced his brother's arrival to almost all of his friends and also to his wife's relatives.

He and his wife offered a dinner in the honor of his brother, Simon Buti. That day was such a big celebration; Mr. Buti's friends came from different directions to greet him. They were curious to meet him. He appeared as tall as Mr. Buti , about six feet tall. In terms of education, he was more educated than Mr. Buti. He was a Scholar, because he was going to become a Catholic Priest from Jesuits denomination.

152

However, he had a strong desire to have children. He said that he had found it very hard to be able to pronounce the celibacy vows. And therefore, he renounced that vocation and ultimately got married. One of his sons became however, a Catholic Priest. He was sent to Italy to further his education. Obviously, he was proud of him, and he spoke highly about his brilliancy and achievement.

Mr. Simon Buti was very happy to meet Bipake and Lunungi. He said that he remembered hearing those names in the Congo. He reported that one of his nephews was employed by "Societé Bipake (Bipake's enterprise). Simon Buti asked Bipake anxiously, "is that your family's business, by chance?" Bipake replied, "yes, indeed, that is my family' business." Mr. Simon shared the news with his brother regarding Bipake's family's relationship with their nephew. The landlord rejoiced exceedingly to hear this association. From that moment on, his trust towards the young ladies deepened immediately from due to that close association. Therefore, every now and then Mr. Simon and the landlord used to stop at the ladies' apartment to chat with them for a while.

Subsequently, the landlord brought up Mr. Magoke's issues, a Congolese man who had become an American citizen for quite awhile. The landlord began explaining to his brother, how Mr. Magoke had ran away with the young ladies' semi precious stones, under the guise of helping them. He claimed he would sell those stones to the best jeweler of New York City, whom he claimed to be a good friend of his. The landlord turned to the ladies, and said, "Ladies you go ahead, and tell my brother Magoke's narrative yourself. Bipake began telling Simon, "Sir, needless to indicate that since Lunungi and I have arrived here, she stopped awhile, and then heaved a sigh and then, shook her head, and said, "talking in terms of challenges, we actually experienced them all." Bipake continued Mr. Simon, from all the negative experiences that we underwent, if we do not learn from them, it would not actually be God's fault, but ours.

In terms of associations, Lunungi and I both spent more time at Lycem, boarding school. We might as well say that we grew up really in the boarding school, and we were exposed to strict rules and regulations. In general, we knew a little regarding how people really behave in society in regard to respect and sincerity. Well, she continued as we had explained to your brother previously, how we actually met Paul Mr. Magoke and his friend Franco Fillipu, who came from unknown place to both of us. As soon as she mentioned Franco Filipu's name, Simon said, "oh, I know Franco Filipu, his father is from the Congo and his mother is from Angola.

So, we know each other's family well; as a matter of fact, I heard that Franco and his family had just returned from America, where he had served as a diplomat. Unfortunately, I was not able to meet him since I was busy making travel arrangements.

Bipake, then continued, Mr. Magoke came in with Franco unexpectedly one day. They came along with our previous landlord in our apartment. We had no idea that they came to visit us at first. We actually were under the impression that they were accompanying the landlord, but subsequently, the landlord introduced them to us, saying that he had just encountered our countrymen in front of the building. They were attempting to get here, however they appeared somewhat confused or lost.

Although, we had been very reluctant at first to meet them, but after speaking to them, during our discussion, we discovered that Mr. Magoke's family had some business associations with my family and Lunungi's family as well. So, we were open to speak we them, now we really regret having taken that sort of approach. Mr. Magoke actually mentioned his relative's name that had done business with my uncle Antoine Bipake. That actually had been the turning point from the negative image to a positive attitude towards Mr. Magoke and his friend Franco. As newcomers, we did not know anybody who could have assisted us to sell our precious stones. Our family's friends, whom we had initially trusted, had failed us utterly. So we had no one else to guide us in terms of selling our stones. Since our cash began to run low, we thought meeting Mr. Magoke and Franco was quite a propos; and naively, we had disclosed our fortune to them. And, we were hoping that they would actually help us to gain our money quickly.

Unfortunately, it had turned out to be a nightmare! Mr. Magoke was so excited, when he saw that double portion of semi-precious stones, from Lunungi and myself. "He suddenly assured us, "Oh, you do not need to worry. You can give them all to me. I will sell them to a friend of mine, who is the best jeweler in the city, and get you the money that your stones worth.

Mr. Magoke, sounded a trustworthy fellow, and he promised to get back to us in two days! Simon screamed, and then, what happen afterward? He asked. Bipake continued, "As we are speaking now, Mr. Magoke had disappeared since that day! We actually made several attempts to reach him at the address and the phone number he had given us. However, the mail kept on returning back to us, stamped "wrong address, or sometimes, it would say "Moved without leaving any address." His phone number had been disconnected. We thought we had an alternative, because we could get his information from Mr. Franco Filipu. Unfortunately when we attempted to reach Mr. Filipu in order to inquire about Magoke, we were informed that Franco had returned to Congo, because his term was actually completed.

Simon was so touched with that sad story. He began rubbing his bold head, because he could hardly understand why would people of the same origin take advantage of each other in the foreign land? He turned to the landlord; he used to address him, as "*YAYA (big brother)," This is how you people treat your countrymen in the foreign land*?" Shortly, Simon continued; "So, the man is really gone forever with your stuff? I am so sorry, to hear this awful story," he added. How embarrassing and disgrace. If the people of the same country could exploit their own people in this manner, but who would help them, Yaya (big brother)?"

He asked. He continued "it is not because I am a religious individual, but people must have some degree of spiritual consciousness in dealing with people. They do not have to forget the *RETRIBUTION TIME MUST COME. WHATEVER YOU DO IN LIFE, THERE IS ALWAYS A PAY*

BACK TIME, SOONER OR LATER! But one day he will be confronted somewhere and somehow. He probably thinks he is smarter than God who created him. Well I tell you, he did not escape, and he cannot, because the World and everything upon it belong to God", Simon concluded. Right after that, the landlord turned to the ladies, and he said to them, "You see, I told you that my brother was going to become a Priest; do you notice how he talks as though he was actually preaching?" The ladies agreed with him, then, laugher! And shortly afterwards, they bade the ladies goodbye.

Mr. Paul Magoke's Re-Appearance

Three months later, after Magoke's incident was related to Simon Buti, amazingly, as it were, Mr. Magoke who had gone for years, decided to visit the landlord whom he knew very well, but did not keep in touch for quite sometimes. He had not been at the landlord's house for about five years.

The landlord also had no slightest idea of his whereabouts. On that particular day, however, surprisingly, Magoke came by, and rang the landlord's doorbell. The clock showed 8:30 p.m. when he appeared. When the landlord's wife opened the door and saw him, she could not believe her eyes.

And shortly after that, the landlord came rushing to the door. I was such a big surprise to him as well, because he could not recall the last time he had seen this man. Joyously, he invited him to enter in the living room immediately. Simon was sitting happily in the living room at that time. The landlord introduced him to his brother, saying, "Simon, please meet Mr. Paul Magoke.

He is Mr. Franco Filipu's best friend." Simon made the connection right away with the story of semi-precious stone, which he had just heard three months ago from the young ladies whom he had just met and who were his brothers' current tenants, next door. The landlord received him in a very polite and happily atmosphere. After being seated, the landlord's wife served him a glass of orange juice, which he had selected from the options she had presented him.

Twenty minutes later, Simon excused himself from the living room, and secretly, he went immediately to knock at the ladies' apartment. When the young ladies perceived him, he was asked to enter the house. However, he answered whispering, "I am here to inform you that there is a guest at my brother's living room right now. He is called Paul Magoke, and my brother had just introduced him to me a few minutes ago. He is a friend of Mr. Franco Filipu," my brother confirmed.

He continued I cannot stay longer here. I must go back to the living room in order to continue having conversation with him. "Bipake and Lunungi insisted for Simon to confirm his statement. Simon said, "It is better that you come in person and verify the fact." Having said this, Simon slowly returned in the living room.

As soon as Simon had left, and return to the living room, anxiously, Bipake and Lunungi rushed to get themselves ready in order to view the guest in question. As soon as the doorbell was rung, Mrs. Buti came to answer. She had a big smile when she open the door and saw the young ladies. Their decision was, if it is really Magoke, we will not give him a chance, we will confront him before everyone without any reservation. We have a great regard for him, but he proved that he actually does not deserve any respect from us.

As soon as they were given access, Bipake took the lead, both of them rushed in the living room. They greeted everyone in the room, and then, they turned to Mr. Magoke whom they recognized immediately. Simon acted diplomatically, as though he did not know anything about the story. Everyone was watching that scenario. Suddenly, Bipake and Lunungi said to him, "Oh, Mr. Paul Magoke! We meet again after five years!

Is this really you? Whatever happens to our semi-precious stones, Mr. Magoke? Didn't you promised us that you would actually come back within two days, and bring us the money, which you were supposed to receive for selling our semi-precious stones? Can you possibly give us that money today?" They asked him, anxiously?

Apparently this situation was too much for Magoke to grasp. Suddenly, he placed the glass of orange juice, which he had been holding on the table, nervously! Mr. Magoke could hardly believe his eyes. He was all confused! He was surprised! He actually thought he was having a nightmare. His replied anxiously: "Oh, ladies, you have moved in here now? Oh, I have no idea that you actually knew my friend, Buti. Oh, please, oh, please, he repeated, oh, listen, *"WE'LL CHAT IT OUT LATER!" HE WHISPERED, "PLEASE STOP THAT STORY! SLOW DOWN YOUR VOICES. WE WILL CHAT IT OUT LATER! PLEASE STOP THAT STORY. HE PLEADED. " OH, I AM ACTUALLY HERE TO VISIT FRIENDS. I DID NOT KNOW THAT YOU KNEW MR. BUTI.*" Do you live here now! Magoke acted nervously. He appeared disoriented, and he could not get his acts together. Every one else was just curious to watch his actions as a result of his mischief; and especially, for having disappeared for such a long time, from the young ladies' view. Everyone in the room was actually observing Magoke's movement.

The girls were stern indeed. They were not playing game with him, because he had been deceitful. Shortly after that, Magoke excused himself to use the bathroom. However, he took longer in the bathroom than it would have been under a normal circumstance.

Those in the living room were murmuring and mumbling about Magoke's reactions. Bipake and Lunungi waited patiently until he came out of the bathroom. He was sweating all over his body. He came out with a napkin in his hand, removing the sweat. Eventually he was frightened. He knew that the girls could've had him arrested in order to revenge for his misconduct.

In order to dissipate that negative atmosphere, the landlord's wife asked Mr. Magoke to continue drinking his orange juice. He then took one or two more sips, and turned to Bipake and Lunungi, saying, "Here is my business card. I am in New York just for business activities. I am actually staying at the Pennsylvania Hotel in Manhattan. You may actually come in tomorrow at 12:00 p.m. and we will have a serious discussion regarding this matter.

Bipake and Lunungi asked Mr. Magoke, "How can we be certain that you would actually be present tomorrow at this place, based on what happened in the past?" He replied anxiously, "Please be certain that I will be waiting for you there. I am actually going to live with you one item from my bag, which you will have to carry, and give it back to me tomorrow. This is to re-assure you that I will actually be waiting for you. He actually left one pair of his eye glasses and one book he had been reading. Everyone present acted diplomatically, trying to encourage the ladies. Well, Mr. Buti said, "If he said that he is going to be there, he probably will. You can give him a benefit of the doubt by actually going to his hotel as he just said!"

Magoke's moral was certainly disturbed. He blamed himself for coming to visit Mr. Buti. He wondered since when those ladies became Mr. Buti's tenants. He had left them at the Haitian landlord's apartment. Mr. Magoke had no slightest idea that the ladies knew Mr. Buti. Nevertheless, he could not escape this time. In effect, the ladies went to meet with him at the Pennsylvania Hotel, the next day. Upon arriving, they saw him with his girl-friend at the lobby getting ready to go to lunch.

As soon as he perceived them coming, he stopped suddenly, and told his girl-friend to excuse him for a few minutes, because he had a short business discussion with his countrymen. It was a short discussion, he said, "I am sorry ladies, I was actually expecting some money transfer from my partner today, however the wire transfers was not performed, eventually. Probably it would arrive tomorrow.

He pointed out to his girl-friend who stood few steps from them, he said, "There is my girl-friend, you can actually verify this fact if you wish. Shortly after that, his girl-friend approached him, and whispered, "My time is actually up. I should get back to work." She apologized and left him talking to Bipake and Lunungi, but she promised to see him that evening, and then left. Bipake and Lunungi question Magoke "So when do you think the money will actually be received?" He answered that, "I believe tomorrow afternoon, the money should be here. He insisted, please come back tomorrow. I will be able to remedy this entire situation. The young ladies, left disappointed. They look at each other and said, "Here we go again with Paul Magoke and his false promise!"

The next day, however, Bipake was not available to meet Mr. Magoke, because she has an exam. So, Lunungi went alone. She saw Magoke in the hotel lobby, and suddenly, he replied, "I regret that the money still has not come in as it was planned. Obviously, Lunungi was very upset to hear that response. Noticing her appearance, Mr. Magoke said to her, let's go to those corner stores, and see whether or not they would accept my credit card, because I do not have any cash available at the present time.

Lunungi and Magoke directed themselves to the nearby boutique. However, the only expensive items, which were pleasing to her in all of those stores, were just a brown full length leather coat and one pair of leather boot, which both amounted to $300.00. Magoke charged the items with his credit card. He subsequently promised to call Lungungi the next day in order to invite her and Bipake to return and receive the remainder of the money. Unfortunately, Magoke failed again to keep his promise. When the girls attempted to call his Hotel and asked to speak with him, they were therefore told that, unfortunately, Mr. Magoke was no longer a guest in that hotel. He actually had checked out of the Hotel since the day before. The day he purchased the coat and a pair of boot for Lunungi was actually the last day that Magoke was seen, and then, he disappeared again forever.

Simon Buti and his brother told the girls, "You see how the world is a tiny, actually is a small planet? You see that no one can really escape completely from his wrong doing on this earth? Who knew that Magoke would one day on his own volition decide to visit my brother after so many years? This is an indication that the world belongs to the Creator, and all of us are held accountable for our acts." Simon Buti concluded. The girls were so grateful to Simon Buti's visit and his wisdom in coordinating the incident diplomatically, which has permitted the girls to confront Paul Magoke.

Chapter IX

Parents' Letters of Encouragement

The latter correspondence the girls received from home was actually signed by their respective mothers, Mrs. Bipake and Mrs. Lunungi. In their church, both ladies held serious responsibilities, and both were members of Women's Congregation. They were viewed as staunch Christians and were very influential. Mrs. Bipake was a deacon and Mrs. Lunungi was a Sunday school teacher. And therefore, the last paragraph of that letter read: "please do not be resentful.

If God forgive all our sins, why should we be allowed to keep grudge? Yes, we would like you to forgive everyone, including Mr. Zariap and Zolog who had deceived you initially. Do not forget, however, that it was because of them that you had chosen to go to New York City, where you are now receiving a good education, which will eventually permit you to become proficient in English.

Further, you should forgive Mrs. Moline, your second landlady, even though she was wrong to steal your white bag containing money, as well as your friends' high school pictures; please, let go of that negative image. Place her in the hands of God.

Furthermore, you also should forgive, those missionaries, Mr. and Mrs., Brown for having been so inquisitive in situations which they have no knowledge about. We understand the degree of your disappointment in regard to their misconduct. It is of course depressing, because everyone regard them highly. Certainly, it is appalling indeed for individuals to conclude that just because they had lived in a country for so long, that they actually had the right to stereotype the citizens of that particular country. How could they forget to remember that every society is composed of diverse level of people?

And yet, they should have noticed it, if they did actually live in the Congo as they claimed there. Nevertheless, you should not be disturbed for their misrepresentation of missionaries' functions. In addition, we do not belong to their church denomination, and therefore, their church could have never awarded you with a scholarship.

Besides, we had also conducted some research about them, and we were told that they did not leave in the city capital either, in order to confirm anything with certainty. They lived in the remote part of the country. Therefore, they knew nothing regarding your families' backgrounds. Nevertheless, we did not send you there to impress anyone or to be mocked by anyone. *Remember what the scripture teaches us, about trials and tribulations; Jesus said: "(John 16:33) I have spoken these things to you so that you might have peace in Me. In the world you shall have tribulation, but be of good cheer. I have overcome the world."* In this accounts, we wish to remind you, their mothers wrote, "Do not attempt to stereotype all the missionaries either, because among them we have seen some, who had really been exemplifying the qualities of the servants of our Lord." So be courageous and remain focused in your studies, also be devoted in the Lord."

In addition to the above mentioned individuals, their mother wrote, "you should also forgive the diplomats for their lack of diplomacy in dealing with those missionaries, and for their failure in handling minor issues. Finally, we would like to advise you also to forgive, even Mr. Magoke, who had run away with your semi-precious stones, nevertheless, had paid it back in Brazil, where he got in trouble with his business associates, and eventually got arrested. This is what has been reported to his immediate family lately."

Ultimately, after the completion of the ESL program, Bipake and Lunungi passed their SAT exam, and were qualified to attend college. Both of them decided to major in the Nursing program. Their parents were able to help finance their studies. They graduated as R.N. and subsequently, decided to returned back home in order to serve at the University Hospital of Kinshasa.

Conclusion

Apparently, human's experience on this Earth was meant to teach individuals lessons from which they might grow physically, mentally, spiritually and morally.

Further, the earthly experience help broaden the individual's knowledge in terms of handling diverse challenges. Probably, various experiences occur so that a person may utilize his or her insight in developing important skills, or abilities to handle various tests, which could appear spontaneously in the future. In life, different occurrence varies with circumstance under which the individual finds himself or herself.

In fact, there may be several reasons why some individuals may appear and connect with a person, sometimes, somewhere, and somehow. Although each experience may diverge in its nature, nevertheless, it is necessary to bear in mind that each one of those experiences is important, regardless to how negative it might appear at that time. In reality, if that individual uses his or her God's given insight, he or she could apparently discover that out of those negative experiences positive elements can be resulted, which could have never been obtained otherwise.

In effect, learning how to forgive and to forget no matter how awful the situation may appear at that particular time is worthy. When you stop dwelling in the negativity, and also refuse to padlock yourself in what other ignorant individuals have done to you in the past, that is when a person can realize that in life nothing actually happens by chance.

There are always relevant reasons why individuals connect with each other, at a particular time. However, nobody can foretell those reasons with certainty, but it could possibly be to reveal things, which may be useful in the future, or to alert an individual to get prepared for any types of future challenges.

Moreover, it is necessary for parents to begin shaping their children, physically, morally and spiritually since their

younger age. Bipake and Lunungi actually began to recall their parents' spiritual advice. In everyone of their correspondence, their parents insisted that it was necessary that they learn to let go of those negative experiences, and then, try to move on. Their parents advised them also that "You could attract God's hidden wealth if you decide to forgive everyone who had been a part of those challenges.

That means, practically anyone who had been unkind to you, whether in your country of origin, or in any other country abroad. Evidently, among of those unkind individuals, you had also met compassionate people who had brought you substantial help such as the gentleman who had helped you at the airport. We were please to read that he endeavored to find you hotel accommodations, and then, an apartment. Besides, he took the time to take to find you a school, and even brought you there to enroll.

We all here are extremely delighted and grateful to that young man, for assisting you with school enrollment as well. Therefore, it is because of that connection that you are now tenants at Mr. Buti's property. In addition, you should remember specially that good thoughts supersede bad thoughts." We have been all taught to begin counting our blessings without fail.

Afterwards, the young ladies felt compelled to forgive everyone who had played a dirty role in all the challenges, they underwent since day one in New York City. Apparently their parents' spiritual advice had contributed significantly in their own spiritual growth, which led them to be willing to forgive and forget those past negative experiences. Obviously, they did realize that out of those negative experiences, came forth certain degree of illumination, which had helped them to become mature and strong enough to cope with serious challenges which they had to face ahead. In addition, the ladies had acquired broad knowledge, which made them capable in helping those whom they met, who were newcomers in this country as well as in the Congo, Africa.

FINIS

BEPONA BOOKS

Africa Presents:

- The Congo RDC and Lingala Language (English, and French version , level 1 – First edition) –
  LINGALA/ENGLISH/FRENCH DICTIONARIES

- The Congo RDC and Kikongo Language (English and French version, level 1 – First edition) – **KIKONGO/ENGLISH DICTIONARY**

- The Congo RDC and Child Education (First edition)

- The Congo RDC and the Congolese Woman (first edition)

- The Congo RDC et la Femme Congolaise (Première édition)

- The Congo RDC and Congolese Cuisine (First edition)

- The Congo RDC and How Tradition Law works in Modern Society (First edition)

- The Congo RDC and Congolese Comedy/Novel

    1. A Mysterious boy called Timo Mikwaya well known as Kamina

    2. A Western Professor with an African University Student

       How Arrogance is like Banana Peel and changed lives

    2. How Can This African Man live with his In-Laws? FOR OVER 15 YEARS!

    4. Experience of Two Young African Ladies in America

    Bepona Collection

NOVELS

Africa presents the Congo RDC and

A Mysterious Boy Called Timo Mikwaya well known as KAMINA

Mr. Aleyi Atondi
How can this man live with his in-laws for over 15 years?

Africa Presents the Congo RDC And
Western Prof. & African Student

ABOUT BEPONA COLLECTION

Our books are written by African descents, particularly from the Congo RDC (located in Central Africa). The Congolese society is composed of the Bantu Peoples and the Pygmies. These authors of African descents had been compelled to share the Congolese culture with those individuals who are interested in diversity. Our educational books are factual.

Generally, Bepona Collection's books are apolitical. We concentrate our books on presenting the Congolese culture, which encompasses general social issues. Evidently, our contemporary history is connected to our ancient traditions. And therefore, we cannot omit touching some other topics, although slightly-sometimes-when we write about Congolese's culture.

Our novels are practically, narrative non-fiction. The names of the characters including the original setting have been withheld intentionally in order to protect the privacy or identities of the individuals concerned.

All our books are written in simple language, terms and style. Our goal is to share our culture and to express ourselves, but not to impress our readers.

KINSHASA, THE CAPITAL CITY THE CONGO, RDC

PRIOR TO THE CIVIL WAR

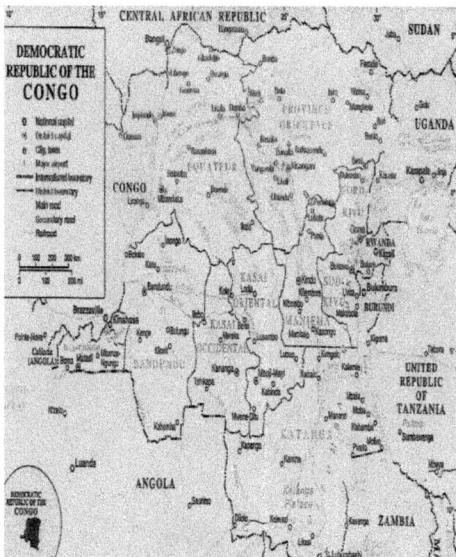

www.ingramcontent.com/pod-product-compliance
Lightning Source LLC
Chambersburg PA
CBHW071438090426
42737CB00011B/1709